SOLDIER BOY

SOLDIER BOY

The Letters of
Gunner W.J. Duffell, 1915–18

Introduced and Edited by
Gilbert Mant

Spa Books

Dedicated to the memory of
William John Duffell,
whom the editor got to know so well
during the writing of this book

ISBN: 0-907590-39-X

Published by:

Spa Books Ltd
PO Box 47
Stevenage
Herts SG2 8UH, UK

Printed in Singapore by Fong & Sons Printers Pte Ltd

Contents

Introduction   7
1   It's Off to War We Go   13
2   Mutiny of the *Berrima*   19
3   The Pyramids and All That   25
4   Prelude to a Bloodbath   33
5   The Big Push   49
6   Please Don't Mind the Mud   60
7   'Every Blooming Thing Is Frozen Stiff'   69
8   The Hot Guns of Bullecourt   80
9   Blighty at Last   86
10   Not to Reason Why   95
11   A Charmed Life   102
12   A Devilish Incense   112
13   From Mud to Mistletoe   118
14   The Depths of Despair   125
15   End of a Perfect Day   135
16   Mary Dircks Gets her Man   143
17   Farmer Duffell   149
Postscript   154
Appendix: The Duffell Diaries   156
Bibliography   160
Index   161

Introduction

The letters, all 153 of them, were found in March 1990 at the back of a workbench in the garage of a home in Port Macquarie, on the mid-North Coast of New South Wales. They were in an old shoe box, littered with sawdust from bench work. The box was tied up with pink ribbon and luckily had tiny ventilation holes in it.

The letters had been written to his family by No 9898 Gunner (later acting Bombardier) William John Duffell during his service in World War I with 2nd and 22nd Batteries, 1st Australian Field Artillery Brigade, AIF. They were now seventy-five years old and some of them were soiled with dried mud from the trenches in France and Flanders in which they had been written, but they were in remarkably good condition, thanks to those ventilation holes. There are wayward spelling mistakes in the letters published in these pages, and they have been left exactly as they were written.

Gunner Duffell had enlisted in late September 1915, a few weeks before his eighteenth birthday. He had served in Egypt, France and Belgium until his return to Australia, medically unfit, in October 1918, a few days before his twenty-first birthday.

A compulsive letter-writer and diarist, Duffell had promised his mother to write home once a week and this he did under all circumstances. He wrote to 'Dear Mother Dad Sis & Bro' at their Sydney southern suburb home at Hurstville, ending with, 'I remain, Your Loving Son & Bro, Jack'. He also made a daily entry in three small diaries throughout his army service, as well as writing numerous letters to other relatives, family acquaintances and a small army of girlfriends. In return, Gunner Duffell received more letters, sometimes sixteen in a day, than any other member of the 1st Brigade and was much envied by other soldiers. As many of the boys didn't get letters, they would be given his to read.

His parents, Lucy and William Thomas Duffell, lovingly kept every one of the letters he sent them and placed them in a shoe box in chronological order.

The war over, Gunner Duffell took the letters with him when he became a soldier settler at Yenda in the Murrumbidgee Irrigation Area. He died there in 1966 at the age of sixty-nine and the old shoe box of letters was passed on to his son, John, a resident of Port Macquarie. He also took possession of other of his father's wartime mementoes: his identification discs, diaries, a jagged piece of shrapnel, old magazines and newspaper cuttings, and a diary recovered from the body of a dead German officer.

As a small boy at Yenda, John Duffell had read a few of his father's letters home, but had not paid much attention to them. At Port Macquarie, he more or less forgot about them. If he did think about them on occasions, he could not remember where he had put them or pondered that perhaps someone had stolen them. Then the day came when he decided to clean up the garage. And there was the shoe box in the sawdust; it had apparently fallen behind a tool box on the bench and on to the floor.

This discovery happened on the eve of Anzac Day, 1990, the seventy-fifth anniversary of the landing at Gallipoli. There was considerable euphoria about the occasion throughout Australia. A contingent of original Anzacs, many in their nineties, made a much publicised pilgrimage to Gallipoli. There was a spate of books, articles, films, radio and television programs about Anzac and the meaning of it all. How and why did it happen? Who was to blame?

Iconoclasts such as Donald Horne and John Pilger pushed the theory that Australians had been led by the nose against their will by the wicked English to fight for the British Empire in two World Wars. Others argued that this was rubbish. Australians went willingly enough because they were of 98 per cent British stock at the outbreak of both wars and they went to war to save Australia from foreign invasion. On the outbreak of World War I the Labor leader, Andrew Fisher, soon to be prime minister, pledged Australia to the 'last man and the last shilling'; in World War II, a conservative prime minister, Robert Menzies, found it his 'melancholy duty' to announce that as Britain was at war, so was Australia. There would have been public outcries had either man acted otherwise.

As a consequence of all this debate so many years after the event, John Duffell perceived that his father's letters and the strange circumstance of their reappearance had suddenly assumed some national significance. He felt it was proper for him to make some of them public.

So extracts appeared in the *Port City Pictorial* magazine in Port Macquarie, and Sydney television presenter Derryn Hinch put some to air on his Anzac Day program.

The letters had a deeper, more personal meaning to John Duffell. He began to read them through for the first time and, as he did so, he grew closer and more understanding towards his father. They had always been good mates in boyhood and adolescence at Yenda, but the letters told him many things he had not been aware of at the time.

He had assumed that his father's regular visits to the doctors were routine affairs for 'returned soldiers'. He did not realise, until now, that his father's purplish swollen legs were the result of 'trench feet', or frostbite, and caused him constant pain. Or that he suffered excruciating and potentially fatal heart attacks, the legacy of a German gassing so severe that it put him out of the war altogether.

The youthful wartime letters of Gunner Duffell were supplemented by a 25,000-word account of his experiences and feelings written by him at Yenda more than two decades later. It is important to consider these two versions together because in his letters he is very careful to spare his family the full horrors of war and to play down his own sufferings and anxieties. However, he pulls no punches in his later version of events, which we will call his Postscript.

The power of the letters lies in their simplicity, a naivety that gradually matures into a kind of shocked realism that reflects the gradual loss of innocence of Gunner Duffell and a more sudden realisation that war was hell, an obscenity. He puts up a protective shield about this towards his family, but the truth is still shattering.

Training in Eygpt with the 18-pounders, he longed for action and live battle. 'I began to wish for the day when those guns would be in action in the game I travelled thousands of miles to play,' he recalled. 'I was young then and had not seen war.' In a Calais hospital with gastritis and enteritis shortly after his arrival in France, he wrote: 'I did not like leaving the battery because I might not get back with them & they will be into the fun in a few days & poor me will be here out of it'.

About the early days in France in a quiet sector, he wrote: 'Not a day passed without some thrilling incident that appealed to my youthful and at that time adventurous nature. I lost that as the weeks, months and years went by.' His self-assurance faltered shortly afterwards, when the Germans shelled and destroyed an orchard in which Duffell's battery had sheltered the night before.

'I'll never forget the roar and crash of those first few shells,' he wrote. 'Much of the glamour of war went out of me there and then . . . Strange as it may sound, but I did not at the period fear for my own safety. It seemed that one must go on playing the game and anyhow one stood as good a chance as the next. I think I was more bewildered than scared.' But a day came at Pozières during the fierce and bloody battles of the Somme when there was a direct hit on the battery by German 5.9 guns. 'From that day on, I was scared,' Duffell noted. The war was no longer a game.

The letters and subsequent postwar narrative tell of the horrors of World War I trench warfare—the cold, the mud, the blood, the lack of sleep, the stench of death of man and beast, the violent noise and savage hand-to-hand fighting, the suffering and death from poison gas.

Through it all, Duffell's creed was: 'Don't worry about me, Mother Dad Sis and Bro, you keep YOUR spirits up. I'll be all right and I'll come home.' He kept repeating this over and over again in nearly all his letters. In fact he seemed to have a supreme confidence in survival and lived a charmed life, outliving two of his gun teams.

There were, of course, happier moments. The letters tell of radiant days away from 'the line' in French villages and farmhouses. Most prized of all, a spell in Blighty, which meant England and a real bed with soft sheets, hot baths, mouth-watering food and the sight and laughter of pretty girls. In particular, he found a 'second home' and a 'second mother' in South Wales with the relatives of a gunner mate. These were happy, carefree times with young people of his own age, even when Duffell was recovering from a gassing. Lots of fun, plenty to eat, walks through the green valleys and hills of Wales, singsongs around the piano at night. Perhaps something deeper might have grown out of his friendship with Cassie Harris, the 'little Welch girl', who vowed to follow him to Australia after the war.

It is not clear from the letters whether Gunner Duffell felt he was fighting for the Empire, though both sides of his family were of British descent.

The catalyst of the Duffell family in Australia was John Robinson, a Scotsman who arrived in Sydney in 1809 as a member of the 73rd Highland Regiment. A new governor of New South Wales had just been appointed, a Major-General Miles Nightingall, to succeed the deposed Governor Bligh and the 73rd Highland Regiment was to go out on the same ship to relieve the infamous New South Wales (Rum) Corps. Nightingall changed his mind and in late April 1809 an officer of the 73rd who had offered his services as governor, Lieutenant-Colonel Lachlan Macquarie, was appointed to that post.

The 73rd Highland Regiment was recalled to England during the Napoleonic Wars and Robinson was killed in the Battle of Waterloo on 15 June 1815. He left behind in Australia a daughter, Eleanor, who married a Thomas Crumpton. Their daughter, Ellen, married John Duffell at Mangrove Creek in 1857. John Duffell had come to Australia from England at the age of three on the sailing ship *Indiana* in 1833. Their son William was Gunner Duffell's father.

Strange, indeed, that Gunner Duffell should have fired his first live shell near Hazebrouck in Northern France in June 1916, fighting with the French against the Germans. He was probably unaware that less than 130 kilometres to the east was the village of Waterloo, where, exactly 101 years before, his great-great-grandfather had fought and died in a famous battle with the Germans against the French.

Despite his ancestry, it is doubtful if Gunner Duffell paid much attention to the survival, or otherwise, of the British Empire. It is much more likely that he felt he was fighting for Hurstville and Australia.

The longer the butchery lasted, the stronger grew his love for 'Ausie' (he spelt it mostly without a second 's'):

I reckon anyone who comes through the next spring offensive will see Ausie and stay there for good. I'll bet no dinkum Ausie will ever leave home again . . . They have not got a six horse team in the army that will get me to live in any of the countries I've ever seen while on this little joke.

At present I am here for the benefit of Australia & my family. Nobody else. I would not give a hang if Fritz took the whole of France & Belgium.

As the war went on, seemingly for ever, it is not likely that Gunner Duffell felt he was fighting for anything in particular. Like his comrades, he accepted the futility and meaninglessness of it all with a dazed kind of fatalism, obeying orders unquestioningly because the job, whatever it was, had to be done. He prayed for a Blighty, dreamed of Ausie, yet when he was away from the line his thoughts were constantly for his fellow gunners at the front. Such is a mateship, forged in war, which no civilian will ever understand.

Like all young men, Gunner Duffell had an eye for a pretty girl. He was a shortish, stocky fellow with dark hair and eyes, and an Australian cockiness that attracted young ladies from the colder climates. There were some pretty little mademoiselles in France and Belgium, but they were only passing fancies. In the meantime, perhaps believing there was safety in numbers, he corresponded recklessly with up to twenty-seven girls, one of whom always addressed him fondly as her 'Soldier Boy'. He regarded himself as a sort of cat among the pigeons and feared for the consequences after the war.

Mary Dircks was different. An eighteen-year-old Sydney schoolgirl, she was a friend of a member of the Duffell family who told her about the young gunner. So Mary began knitting and sending him socks and balaclavas. With each parcel she sent a short note and a photograph of herself. In return, Jack sent back his photograph and Mary fell instantly in love with it.

The socks were a godsend to Gunner Duffell but he did not give much of himself away to her in his polite letters of thanks, though he was once incautious enough to remark to his mother, 'Mary must be a pleasant girl, she writes great letters'. Little did he know that he would meet Mary for the first time on his return to Australia in 1918 and marry her.

Gunner Duffell was badly gassed in November 1917, the poison affecting his heart. He spent seven months in English hospitals before being repatriated to Australia. The first ship he boarded was sunk by a German submarine three days later. He wrote a vivid account of the affair, with a magnificent passage describing an army band sergeant standing on a hatch and playing a silver cornet as the ship slid down to the bottom of the Bay of Biscay.

Duffell was known as Jack to his immediate family, as 'Duff' and 'Gunner' to his army mates and as John to the community at large. For the purposes of this narrative, we will call him Jack as he prepares to go to the 'war to end all wars'.

1

It's Off to War We Go

The future Gunner Duffell was the first child of William Thomas and Lucy Elena Duffell, boarding-house keepers of Hurstville, a southern suburb of Sydney that was still a small rural community at the time of his birth. Nearly everyone was a Methodist because that was the only denomination available in the district. The nearest hospital was at Glebe, an inner-Sydney suburb, and that was where William John (Jack) Duffell was born on 10 October 1897.

Hurstville then was described as a 'very pretty suburb, rapidly increasing in favour with those who can afford to have country residences within easy reach of Sydney'. When the first white people came, it had been a district covered with magnificent forests of gum, stringy and ironbark, and turpentine trees. The rugged bushland stretched down to the mangrove swamps of the Georges River. Until the early 1800s it was left to the Aborigines, apart from hunters and the occasional escaped convict.

With the coming of white settlers, the district had slowly developed into an area of dairies, piggeries, poultry farms and market gardens. In 1887 it was incorporated as a municipality, whose operations started with two men, a cart and a horse; it was not until 1896 that council decided to buy a bicycle for the town clerk so he could collect overdue rates. Even as late as 1921, the Commercial Banking Company of Australia sought permission to erect two horse-hitching posts in front of their banking premises. At the time of Jack's birth, the population of Hurstville had only recently passed the 1,000 mark. The dairies, the piggeries and the market gardens were still there. Jack grew up with plenty of open space around him. The Duffells lived in a big house with enough ground to run poultry and grow their own vegetables and fruit. (Today Hurstville is one of Sydney's major commercial and shopping centres, with a population exceeding 70,000.)

Jack was a normal Australian boy of his period. Short but stockily built, he possessed a cheeky kind of self-assurance and independence, but very little knowledge of the outside world, let alone a remote place called Bosnia in Central Europe. His world was Hurstville and his mates. He attended Kogarah Public School where he was an average student but very good at all kinds of sport.

So the assassination of Archduke Francis Ferdinand of Austria in Bosnia in June 1914 was of very little interest to Jack and his mates. He had recently left school and was looking forward eagerly to a special party his parents had promised him for his seventeenth birthday. He had a safe job as a packer with Gollans, the big Sydney wholesale firm, but was looking around for something more rewarding and congenial. It was not long before Jack knew where Bosnia was—the bullet that took the Archduke's life exploded into World War I by 4 August.

There was wild patriotic enthusiasm at first in Australia. Recruits flocked to join the newly formed Australian Imperial Force (AIF) to fight for King, Country and Empire. However, things went badly for the Allies on the Western Front for the remainder of 1914 and the Germans advanced to within a few kilometres of Paris. The Allies counterattacked on the Marne River and drove them back. The struggle developed into a bitter and bloody stalemate of trench warfare throughout 1915.

In the April of that year, troops of the AIF went into action in the ill-fated Gallipoli campaign. Though accounts of the savage fighting and heavy Allied losses were watered down by censorship, Australians were jolted by the appearance of long casualty lists. The public were also horrified by the sinking of the unarmed liner *Lusitania* off the coast of Ireland by a German submarine on 10 May. It was torpedoed without warning, with the loss of 1,457 lives. Gallipoli and the *Lusitania* aroused a new wave of patriotism and anti-German sentiment. Enlistments doubled, but the news from Europe, Gallipoli and the Eastern Front continued to be bad; it was described as an 'hour of danger'. In mid-June 1915, the British government told Australia it wanted every available soldier. Renewed recruiting drives were launched.

Jack Duffell was caught up in the fervour and excitement of the moment. The age limit for enlistment was eighteen to thirty-five years but one or two of Jack's mates had fiddled their ages and joined up. He pleaded with his parents to be allowed to do likewise. They were adamant that he must wait until his eighteenth birthday in October. He spent the next five months fretting that the war would be over too soon and he would miss the 'fun'.

It is not clear how he managed it, but his official date of enlistment of 23 September 1915 was seventeen days short of his eighteenth birthday. He was sworn in at Victoria Barracks, Sydney, with three other Hurstville mates—Frank, Bob and Fred.

The war had been going on for fourteen months when Jack enlisted. By the end of it all, in November 1918, more than 42 million soldiers had fought on the Allied sides against 23 million from the Central Powers—Germany, Austria–Hungary, Turkey and Bulgaria. The allies had lost 5 million lives. Three million were from Russia and France and 60,000 from Australia, with a population of only 4.5 million. Enemy losses were 3.4 million, 3 million of whom were German.

The Hurstville boys joined 150 other recruits quartered at Victoria Barracks and were drafted into the 13th Reinforcements of 1st Australian Field Artillery Brigade, then serving on Gallipoli. The recruits were put through initial foot drill before beginning their real training as gunners. Jack wrote in his Postscript: 'It was with pride and not a little awe that I took my seat on an 18-pounder gun and spun the dial sight and clino [clinometer] to the commands of old "stripey", the sergeant-major whose lot it was to knock gun-laying into our thick heads'.

Their schooling was elementary in Australia before being sent to Egypt for further intensive training. They were moved from the barracks to a tent camp at Warren in western New South Wales before being given final leave and embarking overseas on 17 December. Jack recalled the occasion in his Postscript:

That day dawned cold & drizzling rain damped our uniforms & to some extent spirits as we marched to Woolloomooloo where the S.S. Berrima was berthed.

A last Mothers kiss at the gate of the wharf & I walked aboard the ship was was to be the home of 700 troops during that long voyage.

As the last rope came away our ship slowly moved into the harbour amid the tunes of brass bands & farewell shouts from the hundreds of good old Australian loved ones we were leaving.

The streamers held by those on board to those on the wharf quickly parted & contact with Sydney was broken.

My thoughts were—will I ever see those loved ones again?

Thus Jack Duffell went off to a war that, in the next three years, was to account for the lives of 8,400,000 soldiers and countless millions of civilians. The immensity of it all could not have been comprehended by an eighteen-year-old boy soldier from Hurstville, or by anybody else for that matter.

Jack wrote the first of his letters home on the following day as the *Berrima* rolled and tossed in heavy seas off the New South Wales coast. He had begun his overseas war service ingloriously. He was seasick— but so were the rest of the troops—and it did not prevent him from writing home, a habit that was to become compulsive:

> At Sea
> 18/12/15

Dear Mother Dad Sis & Bro.

Here I am again after 24 hours sickness I started leaving the heads and am only getting about now but I am lucky for a lot of the fellows are still down. Fred is next worse after me but Frank and Bob were only slight. We had very rough weather last night, she stood on end time after time. The wind tore through the rigging like thunder. I was in the stern wheelhouse sick as a dog & at 9 o'clock P.M. I tried to get down to the mess deck 3 floors down, the first one I fell somehow & when I did you talk about a mess deck I'll bet it was nevver in such a mess before the hammocks were hanging up but very few could get in them. I managed to get in one with the help of John Polson & slept a night of misery till this morning. Now I am well again so I will enjoy the trip. The sea is calmer now and the rain has stopped so it ought to be nice.

There is not much news so you must excuse this small letter. We are not calling till Freemantle rotten luck again. A Pilot boat is coming to take these letters as we pass Melbourne but we are not calling there. Did you get the letter I sent yesterday we wrote them & put them in a bottle & threw it to a launch to post them. We were anchored in stream for some hours & launches came around us all the afternoon & we saw Laura Swanson on one. Well all I will close this short note now as tea is ready & I am going to have some being the first meal I have tackled since leaving. So Goodbye for the time being & dont worry.

> I Remain
> Your Loving Son & Bro.
> Jack.

He wrote a second letter on Christmas Day from 'Somewhere in the Pacific'. According to Jack, the ship could easily have reached Fremantle in time for Christmas but the authorities had deemed it prudent to hold the festivities in mid-ocean:

Somewhere in the Pacific
25/12/15

Dear Mother Dad Sister & Brother

Here I am again about 98 miles from land and I am still as well & as happy as I can be. I hope you are all the same. . .

We have had a very long and tedious voyage so far & not called at either Melbourne or Adelaide. They took us on a track right away from the usual course. We have not seen land since we left the NSW coast & that was 7 days ago & we are over 200 miles out. For some reason or other they wanted to keep us out of port for Xmas so we have taken about 10 days instead of 7. We should have got to Fremantle on Xmas Eve but the heads thought we ought not, so here we are 100 miles from anywhere on Xmas day.

Last night we had a grand concert that lasted till midnight. The crew made up as nigger minstrals & the like & of course we had Chas Chaplin. I think it was the best show I have seen for I enjoyed it right through. There are some chaps here of the stage & I'll bet you would not find 3 better men at comics. Singers are like flies and some are real good. . .

I have just opened the Xmas pcl and you just want to see the four of us. We are in a lifeboat & from the canteen we got 2 bottles of fruit salad, some soft drinks & chocolates. It is as good a spread as you could wish for & I thank you all for thinking to put the pcl in. We are keeping the pudding for dinner.

For breakfast we get porridge & then steak or lambs fry stew or chops. For dinner we catch soup & then roasts & vegetables we have had rabbit twice so as you see we live high. I am getting as fat & lazy as a pig. When we get to Eygpt we will be too fat to work at this rate. . .

On Sunday we had a church service on deck. I think all enjoyed the service. It seemed so strange having church way out there in mid ocean. We are having another this morning.

We go about in bare feet & climb up everything we come across. We will think we are sailors if we keep going. The other day we started up the main mast but when we got about half way up we were informed that we would get 14 days if caught up there. Of course we took a long time to come down (I don't think).

There is great fun between the chaps who had their hair cut off & the ones that have not. A good number of chaps had their hair taken off when we left but the others are waiting till they leave Australia, so you see the short haired mob often catch one of our mob & clip him, the only trouble is they leave a big patch on top. So far we 4 have kept ours. . .

The porpoise play around the ship. I have not seen any whales myself but 3 came close to us a few days ago. The albatross follow us all the time there is about a dozen of them always flying about. Of course we sleep in hammocks & funny it was at first to watch some of them getting in them & very often on to the floor with a bump.

Well dear ones I have just returned from the church service it was nice & it helped us think we were nearer home. The minister preached a nice sermon & told us we were thought just as much of & we could be happy even if we are on the sea on our own.

We have just had Christmas dinner & what do you think we had? Roast pork & beans with spuds & lots of plum duff to finish on. We were that full that we could not eat any of your pudding but we will make it look small before the day is out . . .

We have just had a rough go with the short haired mob. They came down in a body of about 50 & Frank was the nearest to them. As soon as they grabed him he hit out & got away. We got to them with mops & mugs & sticks & in the finish they left us. I was upended in the fun but I still have my hair. They make a mess of any hair they clip. When we leave Freemantle I will have mine off not before . . .

27/12/15 8 a.m. We have just entered Freemantle harbour so I must say Ta Ta for the present. I will write when we get into camp. Everything in a hustle & rush so Goodbye again & don't forget that I am well & do not worry.

> I remain
> Your loving Son & Bro
> Jack
> X X X X

2

Mutiny of the *Berrima*

The *Berrima* steamed to Fremantle non-stop and there Gunner Duffell found himself 'in action' sooner than he had anticipated.

The ship was to stay at Fremantle for some days loading wheat and it turned out to be a lively interlude for the 700 troops who disembarked there and were sent to the Blackboy Hill military camp, about twenty kilometres from Perth. They immediately ran foul of the Western Australian commander, a Colonel B———, who by Jack's accounts had a great aversion to 'Easteners', especially those from New South Wales. There are two versions of the mutiny and riots that ensued, one rather emasculated account in Jack's letters home and the other in his recollections written a quarter of a century later.

It appears that Colonel B objected to his camp being befouled by the presence of New South Wales soldiers and took action to make their short stay there as uncomfortable and unpleasant as possible. He refused them leave, sent them on route marches to 'keep them fit' and gave them food, mostly stew, that Jack described as being 'unfit to eat'. 'This camp is an awful place and they treat us like dogs,' he wrote home. 'The colonel calls us everything that's bad.'

After about a week of this treatment the troops went on strike. Refusing to eat the food or go on route marches, they walked out of the camp and found their way to Perth by various means. Colonel B responded by cutting off food altogether. The climax came when they started to break camp again, only to be met by about 600 Western Australian soldier picquets with fixed bayonets, led by six mounted officers. Jack wrote to his parents, describing what happened next:

There were 1300 of us [this figure conflicts with his earlier roll-call] and we all got together and charged the officers. We beat them back but the bayonets took some beating. We all got together to make a final charge when Major Gallagher arrived. He asked for silence and then asked why we were doing this. He is a grand fellow and when we told him, he had the picquets sent away. He said it was not his fault and pleaded with us to go back. He said he would try to get us leave and fix things up. If we didn't go back, he would have nothing more to do with us but go back to Sydney and that would break his heart.

We told him we would go back till 4 p.m. for his sake but if we got no dinner and no leave then we would riot again. Colonel B went for his life and we were given a good dinner. So you see dears a riot in the right place does no harm.

We 4 Hurstville boys went back to Perth at 10pm and found the town in an uproar. The boys had got more beer than was good for them and were smashing up the Greek and German shops. They had all the picquets out but they were no use because the crowd were on the NSW side. A lot of Greeks took their things out of the windows & washed them to make the place look empty but that did not stop the boys for they broke all the windows.

We kept right out of that because there is no use in running wild & getting a bad name for nothing. But if we get the Colonel before we go, God help him for he caused all our trouble in camp. He told the picquet to pin every man who tried to pass. He said he would break the NSW men's hearts. But let the boys see him. They tried to burn down his tent last night.

In his postscript, Jack describes the first break-out in more detail:

It was not many hours before the Berrima boys, became hostile and decided to break camp & make for Perth. It seemed the only thing to do seeing that applications for leave had fallen on deaf ears.

Theer was of course a guard on the gate but what could he do with a force of 700 angry men? Anyhow being an 'Aussie' he didn't do anything except wish us luck & fair hunting at Perth.

Few managed to get cars to convey them to Perth but hearing that a train was due the majority waited for its arrival & then swarmed all over it. The engine driver refused to move the train until some half dozen with knowledge of steam engines threatened to take charge. The poor man then had to either leave his engine or take the train on. He went on to Perth. Astonished but helpless ticket collectors were told to book the fares up to Kitchener & 700 men set off to take in the sights of Perth & buy a meal, something the Colonel at the camp had not done for us.

For the most part the troops were very orderly & by lights out that night were back in camp. Next day of course Colonel B had something to say regarding the events of the previous day.

His remarks were so pointed that at once he was counted out in no uncertain manner & once again the whole 700 'Bad eggs from the Eastern states', rushed the now strongly guarded gate & forcing the guards gently aside set out for Perth or where they liked.

For 5 days this went on, but on New Years Eve something started the boys & in the ensuing riot a couple of Greek shops together with a German Hairdresser & Tobacconists were broken up. This was rather a sorry ending to our last day on Australian soil & last day it was because on the following morning 1st of Jan 1916 we were ordered to embark on the Berrima again. By 7 pm the last sight of our dear Australia had faded from sight, out of the sight of many for ever. But what a day the last day had been & it could have all been avoided had that Colonel used the tact common to most Aussie Officers & so lacking in himself.

There was a comic aftermath to this affair, related by Jack in a letter home some weeks later: 'I forgot to tell you about the cocky the boys pinched from the rotter colonel at Blackboy Camp. When we got back to the ship they taught the bird to say awful things about its old master. One day when the Major was going his rounds he stopped to talk to cocky & he left fly some of the vilest language about Colonel B that the Major was shocked.'

Jack also heard from some later reinforcements that squads of Western Australian police with fire hoses had awaited their arrival in the streets of Perth, expecting similar trouble from the troops. 'You need not be afraid,' Jack assured his parents. 'I won't get into trouble for I see by the letter you were anxious.'

The *Berrima* steamed off into the Indian Oean towards a 'secret' destination but it was common knowledge that they were headed for Egypt, where large British forces were in training. On New Year's Day, 1916, Jack decided to keep a daily diary and this he did until his return to Australia in October 1918. The diaries are still in good condition and there is an entry for every day. (Extracts from them are shown in the Appendix.)

Jack wrote only two letters home during the voyage, which was uneventful. Although they do not contain anything of great import, they reflect the young man's constant excitement and fascination as new sights, sounds and people came within his orbit. He wrote it all down in such simple, almost naive language, that it painted a clearer, more authentic picture than more highfalutin words might have done.

There is no indication in the letters that the men of the *Berrima* were aware that, seven days after they sailed, their Anzac comrades had evacuated Gallipoli and were also heading for Egypt.

At Sea.
14/1/16

Dear Mother Dad Lily & Tommy.

Just a few lines again to let you know that I am still well & as happy as can be expected. I do hope & trust you are all well & are not worrying about me. Since we left Fremantle we have not seen land and things have been very slow. The weather has been very tireing. I think I will melt away if this keeps on. Some days we get about in shorts only. To see us you would think we had turned into heathens.

Today Fred & I were hanging over the side catching the spray & talking about the times we used to have & to us it seems months since we left but won't we make up for it when we come back. It is Sunday today & we had our usual church parade this morning & the rest of the day we have been letter writing. Last Wednesday we started a boxing tournament & some of the boys put up a good show. They had 4 chaps blindfolded in the ring together & they went it hammer & tongs. One chap got over to the corner where the officers were sitting, the first one to get knocked was the Chaplin then the Chief engineer stopped one. When the chap saw who he was hitting you should have seen his face.

On Wednesday night we had another concert & everyone enjoyed it. We were inoculated again on Tuesday and this time they gave us a double dose witch resulted in many sore arms. Mine was bad for 2 days. This last few nights it has rained & all the top decks sleepers have been hunted down stairs to sleep, so we are rather crowded up at times. Arguements are brisk. When we cant do anything else we argue the point about anything.

I am keeping the diary from the first of the year, but there is not much to put in it so far. News is not to plentiful out here but when we land I expect to be able to tell you something. How are all the friends & relations give my best wishes to any you see please. I am writing to some of them but I can't write to all. Much as I would like to. How did you spend Xmas & the New Year holidays. Have you still had friends coming to help you keep your pecker up. I still have the piece of colour I waved with. Keep your half & when I come home we will make something with them. Tell the little ones that I am always thinking of them & how I miss them. I am keeping my end up & also my pecker but I can't help thinking how I would like to see you all again. But with Gods will I will have you all around me again. That is after we have dished up all the Turkish artillery.

Well dear all I must close now & I will post this at the first port we call at. We don't know how soon we will touch that is why I have written so early. So good night dear all & please remember that I am well & do not worry.

P.S. Have just sighted   I Remain
east coast of Africa   Your fat Son & Bro,
16/1/16   Jack x x x x
wont be long now

                             At Sea
                             Entering Red Sea
                             18-1-16

Dear Mother Dad & Sister & Brother

Here is your boy again as well as I have ever been & almost as happy. You are all well I hope & I know you are not worrying because you told me you would not. You see we are now nearing the end of our voyage in fact we expect to land next Saturday. We entered the Red Sea today & are seeing all sorts of strange things. We sighted land for the first time since leaving Fremantle on the 15th. It was the east coast of Africa & a rocky coast it is. We passed the Arabian coast last night & this morning we passed Islands at the mouth of the Red Sea. Holds gates are names of them. They are more like Hells gates in this heat. We have picked up a war ship for escort at last. Up till now we had none. I am going to send this letter on to England by one of the stewards to be posted there. That will save the censor scratching out every little thing. I dont know how long it will take to get to you. I hope it wont be long. I have written to Aunt Mary & about 12 of the friends & relations so they cant say I forgot them . . .

We crossed the line last Wednesday at 12 a.m. While in the tropics the sun was unbearable but we were naked almost. The heat did its worst on a lot of the chaps. Skin came off them in inches. Over here everything is different to your side of the line even the flying fish & porpoise have changed. We saw some porpoise on Wednesday about 10 ft long & pure black. There was about 100 in the school. The flying fish look nice when they rise in a shoal & the sun shines on the different colored wings. Sometimes they are thick, some red some blue or green. They are all black (*your*) side. The sea is dotted everywhere with small islands there are about 12 in one group & a light house in the middle. They are pure white & look a lovely sight. Yesterday no less than 17 ships passed us but when we were out in the unknown we saw about 2 a month.

We still have the church parade of a Sunday & the boys all make for the best positions to hear the service. I wrote to Mr Medcalf & told him I suppose he will think we were not so anxious to go to church at Hurstville. How is things at home. I hope Dad is still working. Has he finished his barrow yet? I expect the boy is getting on well. Does he remember Jacka yet? I often think of him & Lill too. Tell her I want her to be good & help Mother all she can. I will try & get some souvenirs when we reach Egypt. Well dear all I must close now & hope you get this soon. Ta Ta for the present & remember me to all the friends Tell any you see to drop a line as I would like to hear from some of them.

Well Bye Bye
I Remain
Your old Son & Bro
Jack. X X X

3

The Pyramids and All That

The men of the *Berrima* landed in Egypt on 23 January 1916, and went into the Zietoun Military Camp just outside Heliopolis, eight kilometres from Cairo. They joined an ever-increasing army of Australian reinforcements and the Australian divisions withdrawn from the Gallipoli disaster. These included batteries of 1st Australian Field Artillery Brigade. The gunners had had a rough time at Gallipoli, some being sent to assist at the British landing at Cape Helles. Also, the Anzac beach, where the Australians had landed, had proved unsuitable for field artillery.

After a year of defensive trench warfare in France and Belgium, 1916 was to be a year of crisis for the Allied forces everywhere. The Germans had sent the Russian forces reeling on the Eastern Front. This, allied to the release of strong German forces from Gallipoli, caused the British government acute anxiety as to a Turko–German onslaught upon Egypt. General Lord Kitchener feared that the East would 'become ablaze' and that the war could be lost there.

So it was planned to leave the Gallipoli Australian and New Zealand troops and their new reinforcements in Egypt to guard the vital Suez Canal. By late April, however, the cool season in Egypt had ended without the Turks having made any attempt to advance across the Sinai Peninsula from Palestine. The danger of any overwhelming attack seemed over for the year and the Turco–German threat to the Canal dwindled. Events on the Western Front, moreover, required the urgent transfer of the Australians to France. Jack Duffell's prediction (via the army's 'latrine news') in a letter that he would be at least twelve months in Egypt was to be very wide of the mark.

Jack and a couple of his mates were drafted to look after the horses and mules, while also receiving battery and gun drill. Each day they were marched into the horse lines to be instructed by a sergeant-major who at one time had broken horses on an Australian cattle station. The training was hard but saddle-work suited Jack, though he pined to be in the fray, aiming shells against the Huns and the Turks. The days were never dull as the sergeant-major led them hurdling over mud walls and on mad gallops across the desert. 'It was grand sitting behind a galloping team,' he wrote home:

We are camped on the edge of the desert. There is sand as far as you can see. This morning I was on battery drill as brakesman again & the team I was with bolted across the desert. The lead driver was thrown and injured but the others stuck on. I had to get down & take the lead horses out when they stopped. They are pretty lively & I was glad when I had them out. Some of the horses are pretty rough & these cold mornings they take some handling. The mules are the worst, they kick every time anyone goes near them

Meantime there was Cairo and other places to explore. Jack had never been outside Australia before, his association with other cultures and traditions had been limited to Hurstville and its environs. Some of his first impressions of Egypt and the 'Gyppos' would be regarded as being considerably 'racist' in official quarters today.

Zeitoun Camp
26-2-16

My Dear Mother Dad Sister & Tommy

I suppose you had thought I had forgotten you but you know I could never do that . . . We have been to both Heliopolis & Cairo. There are nice places. Heliopolis is all white. The buildings are pure white & the roofs are made of stone the same as the walls. Cairo is a big city & the main streets are as good as Sydney sts. The back streets are awful. We went down a few to see what the slums were like but we soon got back to the main street again.

The natives are the most god forsaken lot I have ever seen. They go about the streets in almost nothing. You cant walk a yard without a dozen of them hanging on to you to buy something. We have picked up some of their lingo & we give them all of it when they hang round us. On Tuesday night we hired four donkeys and started out for fun. We tried to get away from the natives but the donkeys stopped when the natives sang out. They tried to rook us with our english money but we got into them in the long run . . .

I hope you are as happy as I am. This life is rough but I cant say I dislike it. You know I always like messing about horses & I get plenty here. Well dear all I will have to close up again & I hope you have kept your peckers up. Give the kiddys a kiss for me & tell Lily I have bought her a silk scarf & will send it later when I get some more things. I beat a native down from 20 piasters to 5 for it. Well good night all & please remember me to the friends. Excuse the writing please as I am writing under difficulties.

With best love & a kiss for each from

Son & brother
Jack X X X X

Early in March the four Hurstville boys were split up, much to their disappointment. Jack and Bob remained at Zeitoun but Fred and Frank were drafted as gunners to a camp at Tel el Kebir. The quartet had been inseparable, in camp and on sight-seeing excursions to the pyramids and the Sphinx.

It seems strange that Jack did not mention much about the men from Gallipoli he had come to reinforce. In fact, the words Anzac and Gallipoli do not appear in his letters. Instead, he refers only briefly to the 'Dardanelles scrap' and the fact that some of the men had taken away German and Turkish army badges as souvenirs. It was to be a long time, apparently, before the birth of the Anzac legend.

Jack continued to express his distaste of the 'Gyppos' but was fascinated by the desert and the street scenes of Cairo:

I would like Lill to see all the donkeys & camels there are here. Everything is carted either by camel or donkey. It is nothing to see a string of camels coming along the street. The natives tie them on to one anothers tails & there they are about 20 in a line loaded till you can't see them with green stuff or anything. One of our Officers bought a little donk for 5 piastres (one shilling) & we keep him in the lines. He is about as big as Carpenters Collie & has about twice as much hair on him. We can buy white mice, rats or rabbits on hire very cheap. There is about a dozen white & black rabbits running about the tents. There are also 2 monkeys, 2 dogs and 3 pigeons. The rabbits eat out of our hands.

Jack kept on writing letters prodigiously, sometimes posting eight in one batch to family and friends. He wrote occasional separate letters to his father and his adored ten-year-old little sister, Lily.

Zeitoun Camp
22-2-16

Dear little Sister

I was so glad to get your dear little letter and I am glad you had a happy birthday. I thought of you but I was a long way from you. I am glad you had a nice day at the beach. You did not send me any icescreams or good things that you had. Did you cry when the wave tipped you over? I don't think you would because you are a big girl now arent you. You are getting on well at school. I did not think you could write like that letter you wrote me. Bob, Fred & Frank read it and said you were getting on well. Well Dear little girl I must close now with best love and a big X for you.

I Remain
your big brother
Jack X X X X

In one private letter to Mr Duffell, senior, he gave solemn assurances that he had not fallen prey to the bad women and bad grog of Egypt:

Zeitoun
March 6th 1916

Dear Dad,

Just a few lines in a hurry as it is getting late & I want to drop you a few lines for if the mail closes for 5 weeks as we think it will you wont get any answer to the last note you sent. I was very glad to get your letter & had a smile at it. I guess the garden must be looking A1 by this. How is the motor car going I suppose you have a heap of manure in the old backyard. This morning I helped to load a waggon. We piled manure on till we could not get any more & then the lead driver asked where it had to go & I told him he could tip it in our garden & he said I wish to (Hell) I was back & I would. There is about 6 waggon loads taken away from our lines every day. How would you like it?

They have not sent me looking for V.Cs yet but I am still standing by & Fred is standing by also. Phil says there are dozens of Hurstville boys down where he is & they are just the thing. There is some bad women here but you can rest assured we keep right away from them & the booze also. A smoke now & then is the worst we go. I know Mum will be thinking things but you tell her it is alright you can take my word for that. There is some things done here that you could never dream of let alone see but once was enough for us. It is great to get the returned men on telling their tales of woe some of them have some good yarns

& take some swallowing. Well Dad I must bring this short note to a close but next time I'll try & spread it out a bit longer. So night-oh for the present & keep the flag afloat.

> I remain
> Your cobber son
> John

By the middle of March, it was evident to the Australian troops in Egypt that they would soon be on the move again, to France, everybody believed. On 16 March Jack wrote to his father:

Dear Dad

. . . Fred and I are now drivers in the 22nd Battery of the 1st Brigade. I expect to go away with the battery before long as driver. I think you would look if you happened to see us on battery drill going for our lives over anything & everything. When these nags get going there is some fun. I have had one fall & that was from a single mount going over a wall. I landed on his neck & hung there for a few yards, when I got my mind back I let go and covered up the head but the old gee hoped over me & started home. I was up again & have not been off since. One spill in 2 months is not bad so I won't grumble if I only get one in 2 months right through.

I guess the garden must be looking some class now with the hose & metre going strong. (Have you carried home any manure since from Pyrmont?) We did things in style the last day at Zeitoun. Went to the zoo in a Motor (not one like yours). We got Barney at the wheel & went through Cairo like blazes. We told him not to mind knocking out a few natives for we would knock a lot more when we get going in (Parley Voo). I saw Graham here a few days back & again yesterday he was cleaning up the horse lines (a little come down for him eh?) Well dad I think Ill have to put the stopper on this so Ta Ta for the present with best wishes & a tight hand shake from

> Son John

The next letter to 'Dear old Dad' was undated and written 'At Sea Somewhere':

Here I am again as well as ever & a little bit better. I received your two letters with Mothers & was so glad you are well. I got a bit of a shock when I read about Mum's bad jaw. I was relieved I can tell you when I knew it was only the nerve injured. I do hope Dr Sands is right & if anything to make you think so again spend my pay & have it fixed up

at all costs. I often lay awake thinking about you all & wonder & hoping
you are all well. As you say you often look for the boy in karkie when
Trix barks. Well before many months I dont see why I shouldnt be walking
down that old path. We are on the move again as you see & am now
in the Mediteranian Sea going to ——— knows where. I have a good thing
on though so I dont mind how long it lasts. The only thing is the (Hell
fish) Submarine they are here somewhere & we have to get about in
great life belts. I used to leave mine down below while at work in the
galley but the heads gave orders to crim anyone not wearing them so
I have taken a tumble & lug it about with me. It would cause some fun
if we bumped a torpetoe But never mind wait till we get going with our
penny bungers Ill bet the boys will make up for lost time. I suppose they
will come over later on I saw all the Hurstville boys the night we left
& if getting wished luck does anything Fred & I will come out of it
('dinkum'). How are you getting on at the 'seaside'. I expect there is plenty
doing. Well Dad I must close up now as there is not much to tell so
Ta Ta till we land & then I will have something worth telling you. I am
not sorry to see the last of Egypt anyway & I hope the next stopping
place will be better Ta Ta again

Then came a letter to the rest of the family 'At Sea Again, 23rd March
1916':

My Dear Mother Sister & Brother

. . .well Dears you see I have had another shift. Fred is with me still
but we don't know where we are going too. We left the last camp &
traveled to Alexandera over night & in the morning of the 22nd we
embarked again for a sea trip. Ill tell you more about it when we land
again all I know now is we expect any minute to spot a submarine after
us. If you get this letter you will know we got through alright.

I struck a good job. As soon as we got going a cooks mate was wanted
& I fell in for the job & now I peel spuds all the morning & eat all the
afternoon. The tucker is just the thing there today I had a good steak
for breakfast & roast pork for dinner & for tea there is fish. The boys
down below get stew & bread & jam. So I kid myself some. I don't know
what became of Frank & Bob I expect they will come after us sometime
later so we might see them agagin. Who do you think I saw the night
before we left. I was standing by my kit when I heard someone singing
out for me. I looked round & saw someone coming over with his hand
out but I could not make out who it was. I asked him who he was &
he asked me if I was J. Duffell as when I said yes he said well shake

hands with Jim Duffell. I was so pleased to meet him & he is such a good chap & what do you think? The first thing he asked me was if I was short of money. I thought it was very good of him but I had some all the same so did not take any. I went over with him & saw Don Duffell he was in bed with an enoculated arm but he is well otherwise. It is tea time now so Ill have to close up till after.

Well here we are again just got outside a good tea & am feeling a fullness under the life belt. I forgot to tell you we cant leave them off & it is funny to see all the boys getting round in life belts. I was glad to hear by your letter that you have been going out a bit & I hope the nips will like their presents. Well Mother I must close again as I am wanted.

24th & another start. We have just had a false submarine alarm and you should have seen the fun. I was having a wash when it sounded & I thought I was in for a swim as well but it was only a trial signal. We are having a nice trip the old raft rolls a bit but the weather is fairly good. Im looking over your dear letter again. I see you have got Tommy some soldiers & Ill bet he is right amongst them by this & I expect he has made war on them some. Well dear Mother I must close up now & I will post this when we reach our destination you may be able to see where it was posted & so know about where we are (I think France). Give my best wishes to all please & dont worry about me for Ill be right as rain when we get going & we wont be mucking them up for a while. Ta Ta & I hope you are quite well about what you thought was wrong about your neck.

> With best love & a kiss
> for each
> I remain
> Your loving Son & Bro
> Jack X X X X

Jack's Postscript after the war described the arrival of the Australians in France on 28 March:

Towards the end of the voyage word was received that an empty troopship s.s. Minneapolis had been sunk by a German sub 100 miles ahead of us. It was then that I began to realise that I was in the war zone & being young & inexperienced the fact thrilled me. . .

Early on the 28th March we steamed into a very pretty harbour which proved to be Toulon. French warships of all size and description are anchored there. We only stayed here for a few hours and then out to sea again with Marseilles the objective. Arrived here during the night & at once disembarked & began a ten mile march through Marseilles & out to a village named La Vallentine. It was a wonderful welcome accorded us by the French people. The singing of the Marseillaise by the people was answered with Australia Will Be There from the troops.

4

Prelude to a Bloodbath

Douglas Haig was the son of a Scottish whisky distiller whose Scotch of that name is still a wellknown and popular brand. His whole life was devoted to study of the art of soldiering. He served his apprenticeship during wars in the Sudan and South Africa before becoming Field Marshal Sir Douglas Haig, commander-in-chief of the British forces in France in World War I. A grateful country rewarded him by creating him 1st Earl Haig of Bermersyde, with a gift of £100,000, a large sum of money in those days.

Yet Haig was to become the centre of bitter controversy during the war and long after it, mainly because of the appalling loss of lives during his Battles of the Somme in 1916. His admirers claim that it was Haig's war of attrition and offensive strategy that finally broke the Germans and won the war.

The war on the Western Front had become a stalemate during 1915–16, though the Germans had shocked the world by releasing its first poisonous chlorine gas attack against the British on 22 April 1915. A disgusting greenish-white mist drifted across from the enemy lines, causing dreadful suffering, but to little military advantage. The sides lay deadlocked in a network of trenches stretching for about 970 kilometres across France and Belgium. In some places less than 100 metres separated the opposing lines.

Haig had been engaged in planning an offensive on the Somme early in 1916 when suddenly and unexpectedly the Germans attacked the fortress of Verdun in north-east France, a key point in the French defence, on 21 February. It developed into a gigantic offensive designed to break the stalemate in the west and force the French to sue for a separate peace. The heroic defence of Verdun, one of the most famous sieges in military history, was to continue for nearly six months. The French lost 542,000 men and the Germans 434,000. It proved to be a disastrous failure for the Germans, though the French had been bitterly critical of the British for not mounting an offensive elsewhere sooner than they did.

The relief of Verdun became one of the reasons why Jack Duffell and his mates had left Egypt for France much sooner than they expected. By early 1916, the British Expeditionary Force (BEF) had been in France and Belgium for nearly twenty months, but after the First Battle of Ypres the old British Army, except for its cavalry divisions, had practically ceased to exist. Haig wanted every man and gun he could get for the great offensives he was planning.

At the time of the Anzac Corps' arrival, in March and April, much of the Allies' Western Front, 600 kilometres of it, was held by the French. By April, Kitchener's New BEF held a sector of 130 kilometres as far south as the Somme River and as far north as Ypres. By the end of April, the BEF contained 1,263,000 men and the number was increasing at the rate of 100,000 monthly. These included 40,000 Australians and 18,500 New Zealanders. By July, there were 90,000 Australians in France and a further 90,000 in England.

The Australians were paid a nice compliment by the famous English war correspondent, Sir Philip Gibbs. He described them as 'those bronzed, hatchet-faced, handsome fellows who brought a new character of splendid manhood into the medley of British types'.

France
3/4/16

Dear Mother & all

Just another letter hoping it finds you all in the best of health still as I am glad to say I am still that same. You will get a surprise I expect to know I am over here. We arrived in France on the 28th March & started on a 10 miles march to our camp. We are in about the prettiest spot I have ever seen. Every little space is covered in green grass & little flowers. It is just the opposite to Egypt. We have had some route marches so we have seen nearly all there is to be seen for a few miles round & all I can say is that noone could wish for a better camping place than this. It is nice to see the old mills with the mill streams running through them. Last night Bob arrived close to here but Frank was left in Egypt. Bad luck on him don't you think?

I am trying to pick up some French but it is slow work & not easy

A few nights back five of us walked into a little place for tea. Of course none of us could tell them what we wanted & after we had been pointing down our throats & patting our tummies for about 5 minutes one of the boys went into the kitchen & took 5 plates off the shelf & then found some eggs so he put 3 on each plate & pointed to the fire so the old dame tumbled to what we wanted & that was the way we got tea. Some class arent we?

Well dear Mum I may not be able to write every week now but when I can you know I will. Things are not quite the same as in Egypt & as we are closer to the front things are strict including the censor. I will send a filled service card when I cant write so dont get a shock & think we are in action but all the same one does not know what will happen over here so keep brave & dont worry & I will feel contented 'wont you?' I must close now dear Mum so give my best love to Dad Lill & Tommy please. I am expecting another mail soon as the last letter from home was dated 7-2-16.

Good night dear   XXXX

                    XXXX   With best love &

                    XXXX   kisses from Jack

The brigade was soon on the move again to a camp near Le Havre, where they were equipped for the first time with guns and horses. Each battery gun team consisted of four 18-pounder guns and six horses. The brigade had a complement of about a hundred officers and men and sixty horses. Jack recalled in his Postscript:

The three batteries of the brigade made a brave show mounted for the first time, looking so spick and span with the new equipment.

As we stood to, waiting the order to move off on that memorable afternoon, a storm burst over the lined up teams & hail pelted down on the fresh horses & in 2 minutes teams were plunging & rearing into a horrible tangle. The order, 'Gunners go to the horses heads' sent us to the unenviable task of straightening out the teams. My particular job was controlling 2 officers hacks.

The storm passed over & order was restored & in Battery column we marched away fully equipped & ready to take over the job we had travelled 12 thousand miles to fulfill. By 7.30 that night we were on board a troop train. Guns, horses & all ranks packed like sardines. Through the night we were carried toward the battle area.

We heard for the first time the sound of heavy gunfire which told us the line of action was not many miles away. I watched while puffs of smoke bursting high in the air & in the direction of the gunfire & was informed by an old hand that those bursts were anti aircraft shells being fired at a Fritz plane. Perhaps its just as well that plane did not spot the close packed teams on that narrow road. A short march to an old farm house & there the horses were picketted in two lines & aftering feeding up the men found quarters in a barn & as night fell we curled up on the straw & listened to those distant guns. War was beginning to be a reality.

Rain fell heavily that night & next morning we bogged about in the horse lines. It was not nice work & everyone was very wet by breakfast time. Then some brass hat discovered the fact that we newly formed batteries had never had any target practice with live shell & we were ordered back to Calais by road to undergo a short course of battery shooting.

It was a tin of 'crook' sardines, not a German shell, that laid Jack low, as he related to his father (to save his mother distress) in his next letter:

> Lahore British General Hospital
> Calais
> 26-4-16

Dear Dad,

I have been writing to the Ma all the time so I think its up to you to get one 'dont you' Well here we are or I should say I am in dock for repairs owing to be torpoetoed with a tin of crook sardines & a week in the mud up to the knees & soaking wet into the bargain. On the sixth day I was feeling rather shivery like so I got a tine of sardines & some bread. Well I next got outside them & the sardines got buisy about an hour afterwards. I kept going till we camped that night & then the pains started & all night I spent in style (I don't think).

I was reported sick next morning & there was three others with me so they shunted us off to the above sick bay. For the first day or so I thought I was poisoned but it turned out to be Gastritis & Enteritis so I am not so bad after all. I got the milk ration for 2 days but today they brought in some fish & pudding. So things are looking up. I wrote to Mum as soon we lobbed here but I wassent to good & I did not tell her much. I know Mum will want to know all about the boys sickness.

I did not like leaving the battery because I might not get back with them & they will be into the fun in a few days & poor me will be here out of it & perhaps not get there for a month. This means none of the four together now. Frank is still in Egypt I think & Bob is somewhere in France & Fred I have just left. Oh Hell here comes some more medicine these sisters are hot stuff on the medicine. They look after us well & are very gentle. They are all English so we pitch them a tale about sunny Australia now & again.

I have had a little travelling since I left there havent I. I have been nearly all over France & seen some of the big places. First Marseilles then Le Harve & Calais & about 20 small towns & villages to I will soon know France a bit. Paris is the spot I wanted to see & then Eng. I expect you know the place after that. It is 4 months since I left & it seems like 12 to me especially not getting any letters for a month or more. But never mind keep hoping for the best that is what I am doing . . . Share the kisses out with Mum, Sister & Bro. Good night & keep your peckers up & hope for the best. Ta Ta for the present & a good hand shake for yourself.

I remain
Your Loving Son
John
X X X   X X X   X X X

Jack often railed at the necessity for an officer to censor his letters, but he wasn't so bad at it himself. He remained in hospital at Calais for seven days and then spent a further eight days in a convalescent camp at Boulogne. He told 'Dear Mother & Dad' about it in a laconic sort of way but there is a much different version of it in his Postscript. In fact, he and three mates finished up in 'clink':

It was while in the camp at Boulogne that we four 22nd battery boys met again & incidently were the only Australians in the camp. The rest were Imperial troops & I'm afraid we Australians did not set a very good example. Twice we broke camp while supposed to be filling sandbags on the beach at Boulogne. It was too good to miss, being in a town like that & not seeing the sights.

Twice we were handed over to the guard & locked in the 'Clink'. It was from the same 'clink' we were hurriedly brought on the morning of the 6th of May & informed by an irate officer of the guard that our Major had ordered our return to the unit as it was about to go into action. I believe the C.O. was pleased to be rid of us & we in turn were not sorry to leave the camp to rejoin the battery and mix with Australians again.

Like prisoners we four were escorted to a train & handed a train warrant that would pay our way to a place called Hazebrouck.

If you have read the Introduction to this book you will remember that this was about 130 kilometres from Waterloo, where Jack's great-great-grandfather had helped to topple Napoleon 101 years previously.

From Hazebrouck we had to find the battery & this took a couple of days as the battery had now moved up to within 4 miles of the line.

Finally after miles & miles of walking through rain & mud the battery was reached & we 4 were received back into the fold like long lost brothers.

Now the sound of battle was more pronounced & everything was being prepared for the battery to take over a sector of the line. At dusk on the 13th May the long awaited moment arrived. I was a member of a gun team in a sandbag pit & laid ready for action. How I longed to tug the firing lever & send the shell over to Fritz just to see what would happen. It seemed too quiet for war. It transpired we were in a very quiet sector of the line where nothing much happened. Perhaps Fritz was breaking in his new reinforcements over the other side of 'no mans' land. The Tommies told us they had been in that part of the line for 12 months & there had been very little firing by guns from either side.

Quiet it was for a few days & then someone woke it up. It wasn't right letting a good war go to waste like that. Battery action & were into it. Officers observed the results of the shooting & keen & observant German officers observed our gun flashes & back came a 5 point 9 shell which knocked the rest of the roof off the already ruined old farm house we had slept in for the past 2 nights. I'll never forget the roar & crash of those first few shells. It knocked the glamour of the war out of me there & then. It was an apple orchard where our guns were placed & soon a great smoking holes were appearing where those 5 nines were crashing. Its good night if one of them lands close thought I.

Now came a change of proceedings for me. I was sent to Brigade headquarters to take on despatch work. Brigade was situated midway between its 3 18 pounders & one 4 point 2 Howitzer battery. Four of us, one from each battery took turns at carrying orders, sometimes by cycle or horseback except when running to the front line or support trenches.

France
May 25th 1916

My dear Mother

I am writing again in hopes of catching someone going to England so I can tell you something about myself. Its rotten this censoring business a chap cant tell you anything . . . I was on guard at the guns when I was sent for to go as orderly for the battery at headquarters. They gave me a bike & there I've been for a week carrying despatches about. I have a (tin 'at) Steel helmet to stop shrapnel so the head portion of me is safe. I was thinking of getting a piece of steel for somewhere else & I have a pair of thick sox handy in case I get cold feet.

Well dear Mum I think I told you all that has happened to me up till now & I feel quite safe so don't you worry at all will you dear. Your prears will be answered won't they? Remember that there are hundreds of Mothers who have boys out here & there are plenty I am sure would like to have some here also. (I don't mean Mrs Ws. sort). Bang Bang. there's our boys sending some over to Fritz. Its just tea time too so a few shrapnel pellets will help to digest it for them. I expect he will send us some over shortly but they couldnt hit us if they tried . . . Well dear I think I have told you all the news so I must give the Dad a turn now. Remember me to all the friends & tell them all to write & I'll try to answer them. Its nice to get letters tell them. Each one has something different to tell so I get the lot. Well Bye Bye for the present Mother & just keep a smile going so you won't be out of practice when I get back. I will be a Big Kid when I do for the food is good & of course I'm good too. Love

                                       & best wishes from

XXXXXXXXXXXXXXXXXXXXXX   Jack

Gnr WJD	Frogland
Knocking spots off	25th May 1916
Germans in all directions	

My Dear Dad.

Here I am again having another go at the letter writing business. (I'll soon be some class at it). How are you? I hope you can say just the thing. How am I well I am as well as can be & feeling quite jolley. I don't know why though unless its the prospect of staying up will 12 oclock to cart huns death warrants about. I am not having a bad time you know I feel pretty happy sailing along with me little hat on the side of me head whistling all the old songs I can think off. Theres plenty of dodging to be done for on the way to one of the joints I have to go to most of the houses have taken it into their heads to spread all over the roads(I wonder *why* that is) I was thinking of asking the huns to oblige me by dropping their shells on the paddocks instead of the middle of the road for it causes such a lot of cuss words to flow when a fellow drops into them of a dark night.

We had some fun here last night. Just after tea two other chaps & I were playing with one of the mascots when over comes a 'whis & a bang' just out side the billet. Needless to say we were soon there too. Just as well for over came 2 more & one went through & open door & burst in the stable. The old French johney who ownes this ranch had his only cow tied up there & the poor beggar stopped about a pound lump of shell case behind the right lug. The Vet stitched her up but I don't think she will get over it. Well about us now About 5 or six of us made for the dug outs for they were putting them in rather fast & we thought they were going to put our billet down south

The scrap lasted about 20 minutes & when they knocked off you could see heads sticking up out of every hole in the place looking for the rest. Thank goodness noone was hurt & the billet was not hurt much for only the one hit it I think. They started putting them into a little village about 1000 YDS from here then & we stood and watched the mess they made of it. Of course it was deserted long ago & shelled before also but we could see the places going all directions. One shell put in the right place means one house in the wrong place... Adiew for the present dear and keep the flag flying

> I remain
> Your Loving cobber son
> Jack XXXXXX

Another letter written two days later advised his father about the old Flemish farmer's cow:

Our chaps have been banging away with their guns all the morning. I suppose Fritz will return the compliment this afternoon. Its a case of you have a shot & I'll have one after. I am having a quiet day so far only two trips this morning & no shells coming over. Its like riding about sight-seeing when the guns are quiet. The fields are all nice and green with wild daisies poppies and buttercups in hundreds. They look like huge flower gardens. How you would like to be among them. I bet you would never want to leave the place if you saw it. Of course all the farmhouses have shed their roofs & some of them down altogether so there will be plenty of work for some one. The old cow I told you about last letter had to be shot. She had 11 pieces of shell in her neck...

How would you like to see two aeroplaines having a duel up over your head? When they are not too high we see the whole lot quite plain. When a machine goes up one side lets her have it and the shells burst like bags of white powder all around it. In the night time the flashes can be seen bursting like red stars away in the air. Its a grand sight...

Gunner Duffell in uniform

*The family Duffell
left behind—Mother,
Dad, Sis and Bro—
in the 'little grey
house in the South'*

*Duffell's Final Leave
pass*

LEAVE PASS.

(*Place*) Victoria Bks

(*Date*) 16/11/15

No W. I. Duffell

has permission to be absent from his Quarters from 4 30

o'clock Tues the 16/11/15 until 10 PM PM o'clock

Monday the 22/11/15 for the purpose of going

to Final Leave

J. Steel Lt.

Commanding 13A Reinf

Cassie Harris, the 'little Welch girl'

'Why the Australian Hat Turns Up at the Side'—wartime cartoon by Wilton Williams in the London Opinion

Sausage Valley (or Gully) during the fighting near Pozières in August 1916. All communications led through this valley to the front line. Gunner Duffell made a nightmare bicycle ride through it under heavy German artillery fire (AWM negative no. E2113)

Well dad I think I'll have to cease firing till next week so remember me to any of the old hands you see. Last mail I wrote about 14 letters so they can't say I dont answer the letters can they?

Keep the smile up on Mum and we will take her for some bosker rides wont we.

So long for the present Dad.

Jack was given a few days off from the gun pits and paid a visit to the front-line trenches. The artillery were based behind the lines where life was more tolerable:

Yesteday morning I got into our rear trenches looking around & seeing what trench life was like. Better still today I got right up our front line & had a yarn to some of the old boys. They are fine chaps, there is no doubt won't be frightened by anything. I saw all there was to be seen in about half an hour & I think after all the artillery will do me. . .

Our infantry are the boys nothing can damp their spirits not even a week in the wet. I met a mob today just come out of the trenches & covered in mud & when they got on the road they started joking with the sergeant about making them walk in the wet. That's after a week of it.

Blissfully unaware of a bloodbath that would soon engulf them all, Jack wrote home mainly about food and another more intimate enemy of the soldier—vermin, particularly 'chats', the marauding lice that nested in the creases of their uniforms and emerged to irritate their bodies to distraction.

Although they received good army tucker, Jack (and no doubt his mates) drooled over more exotic food. Jack and another young gunner were camped in a French village and occupied what used to be a pigs' sty. There was just room for two bunks and a table, luxuries to those in the front line trenches:

We live like two kings. We have a small stock of eatables. Most of our pay we spend on tinned sausages, tomato sauce, some anchovy paste, jam, jellies & plum pudding . . . I will be sorry when we go out of action for I am just enjoying the life. Plenty of experiences, good tucker, what more can a chap want?

There is an old Frenchman living in this village he grows all sorts of green vegetables so some of these nights I am going to get in amongst his shallots & lettuces & have some salad for a day or two—Some one pinched about 6 rows of his new potatoes and didn't he roar he was running about singing out Australians par bon (no good). Some of the women back a bit make nice custard tarts and sell them to us. It always reminds me of your tarts when I start on them, Mum dear. . .

Mum Dear wrote back, expressing shocked disapproval over the theft of the old French farmer's shallots and new potatoes. Jack rather lamely justified this by explaining that the farmer had an orchard of fruit but refused to sell any of it to the Australians:

I have stuck some pictures up in our Pigs sty so it looks like home. The eatables department is going strong too. We had stew and kidneys yesterday & plum pudding pineapple & a few other dainties. We may as well spend our money that way as neither of us drinks & smokes are given out so you see we put it to a good use. . .

I intend getting some jellies & setting them in tins that is an easy way of getting a pudding. You won't have much trouble to feed me when I get back for I have learnt a few wrinkles in getting up a meal. Making toast by throwing the bread on the hot ashes & making welch rabbit to put on it or fryed bread. . .

Well dear all here we are again just had a bonza breakfast of porridge & steak so I am feeling full. I have sickened myself of fryed eggs. For about three weeks I used to average about 8 eggs a day & now I don't like them. Of course I still like them boiled & cooked other ways so don't think the eggs are safe when I get back. I would not like to be in the one's shoes that suggests stew for about 10 years though. . . But how I would enjoy a good old Sunday dinner of roast & vegetables with plenty of the old gravey. I'll bet you wont be able to make enough for me when I get back.

The 'chats' worried him all the time and he made frequent requests for insecticides to be included in his food parcels from home:

Next parcel please don't forget some life buoy & Mortien for it is almost impossible to keep free from chats as we call them. They keep us awake at nights & we have to fasten a rope round a gun on to our legs to keep them from running away with us.

By jingo I have had a great time since the night I slept in an old barn for I picked up a choice collection of live stock & they keep me merry trying to round them up. You had better send me a good whip & a sheep dog & I might hunt them out.

I asked you to send me some insecticide some time back so I hope there is some on the way for I can assure you our 'pets' are getting over the odds. They take charge of a chap altogether. The boys call them the second army to fight they are nearly as bad as the huns. . .

I have just had an exciting battle with the other inhabitants of my shirt but they beat me for there is a couple having a hell of a row in the middle of my back. I can tell you they take some shifting when they start . . .

The rats are bad too. They have great times in our dugout at night. One used my face as a door mat a few nights back but I can tell you he got a shock when I woke up. Nearly as big as I did when I felt him crawling over my face.

And in a more philosophical mood, Jack wrote:

You are 10 hours ahead of this side and I often say when I am getting up in the mornings I wish I was in Aust. for I would be going to bed instead of getting out. Of course, today being Sunday we don't fight (I don't think) I was only thinking this morning of the vast difference between these Sundays and the ones in old Hville. Just the same as any other day up here & in many cases I think the saying of better today better the deed for there is some fine old splathers at times . . .

Another personal item in a private letter to Dear Dad was: 'I got a bottle of Eno fruit salts & so I put a little in the water I drink. It ought to keep the blood in order. I have not had many pimples on my face for a long time now as it must be fairly good.' Jack was then four months away from his nineteenth birthday.

There is a significant item in a letter dated 28 June, although Jack was not to realise it at the time. 'I never thought I was so good looking that someone would fall in love with my photo,' he wrote. 'Tell Aunt Jose to put in a good word for me with Mary Dircks.' Aunt Josie must have done so because five and a half years later Mary Dircks was to become his wife.

These dissertations on food, chats and dreams of home were soon to be violently cut short by General Sir Douglas Haig (he did not become a Field Marshal until 1 January 1917).

Summer had come to the Somme district of Northern France that June of 1916 with nature a riot of beauty and burgeoning life. The wild daisies, the poppies and the buttercups were coming to full bloom and the nightingales sang in the leafy places. The wheat was ripening and the beasts grazed placidly in the fields. Only the mad humans of the planet could convert this harmony into a season of wholesale slaughter and despolation.

On 24 June General Haig ordered the softening-up process for his Big Push to begin. A seven-day artillery barrage followed, during which more than 1,500,000 shells were fired at the German positions. Such was the fury of the bombardment the guns could be heard across the English Channel. 'The Big Push was to come at last,' wrote Sir Philip Gibbs:

Trench warfare was to end, and all this great army of ours in France was to get out of its ditches and out into the open and strike. Enormous hope took the place of the doubts and dolefulness that had begun to possess men of melancholy minds. It would be a chance of ending the business. At least we had the strength to deliver a smashing, perhaps a decisive, blow. All our two years of organisation and training and building up would be put to the test, and the men were sure of themselves, confident in the new power of our artillery, which was tremendous, without a doubt in the spirit of attack which would inspire all our battalions. They would fight with the will to win.

5

The Big Push

On 1 July 1916, hundreds of thousands of British, Australian, French and other Allied troops rose out of the trenches they had held against the Germans for nearly two years. They advanced in a great wall across the no man's land of open country towards the most formidable system of defences ever organised by great armies. Thus began a series of the fiercest and bloodiest battles in military history.

Sir Philip Gibbs described it as the beginning of a fiery crusade to destroy the infidel. By the time the Battle of the Somme ended in another stalemate at the end of November, more than a million lives were to be lost with no important result for either side. The lesson was that the technique of defence by both sides had become sufficiently strong to be a match for any offensive force that could be thrown against it.

There are various estimates of the appalling cost in lives. The most likely figure is that the Allies lost about 600,000 men and the Germans 500,000. B.H. Liddell Hart, the noted British war correspondent and military historian, observed that the infantry of both sides 'served as compressed cannon-fodder for artillery consumption'.

The Anzac Corps of Australians and New Zealanders was on the left flank and the main agent of Haig's new plan of 'methodical progress'. Fighting with immense courage and determination, they suffered grievous casualties. Names such as Pozières, Bullecourt, Villers-Bretonneux, Passchendaele, Amiens, Mouquet Farm and the Hindenburg Line have become part of our military folklore. More than 23,000 men were expended in these efforts for a gain, after six weeks, of a tiny tongue of ground just over 1,600 metres deep. The artillery bombardment at Pozières lasted for sixteen hours before the Australians occupied the position.

Liddell Hart quotes from the last letter of a gallant Australian soldier, Lieutenant J.A. Raws, speaking of the 'murder' of many of his friends 'through the incompetence, callousness and personal vanity of those high in authority'. Others would say that this was the price that had to be paid for ultimate victory. Liddell Hart also quoted from another Austraian officer: 'We have just come out of a place so terrible a raving lunatic could never imagine the horror of the last thirteen days'.

Teenaged Jack Duffell was but a microcosm of the hundreds of thousands of soldiers locked in this death-struggle. His letters were fewer in the early weeks of the Big Push. One can conjecture that he was too busy at his guns to write home or that the censor had been busy again. Fortunately, his Postscript fills in the gaps and gives a vivid account of the slaughterhouse of the Somme. He found time, however, for a letter to his father on 23 July, three weeks after the Big Push began:

France 23/7/16

Dear Dad

just a letter all to yourself as this last few letters I have not had time to answer both Mums & yours. Today there is a lull so I am taking advantage of it to write a couple of letters. I am pleased to hear you are all OK. I am myself & still contented with my lot. You see we are at them again & this time it is a great deal hotter than the last position. I am at the guns & have just taken off my boots for the first time in 3 days so you see we are pretty busy (stocktaking). I suppose you have seen in the papers the good work the Australians have been putting in since they came to France. I'll bet Fritz is sorry we came. I like to see the boys bringing in the captured sausage mongers after a charge. But by what I see of it they don't mind being caught. There are plenty of curios laying about here as this was German ground a week or so back. I wish you could see some of the things & sights we do I am sure it would open your eyes somewhat. Grand sights as well as awful ones.

Of course we get our share of his shells but that is all in the game & I reckon we always give more than we get. I can't tell you much you know but under the circumstances I reckon we have done well & are a lucky lot although it was on a 13th day that we took the field first. There is still a lot of the old 13th left but some of them I am sorry to say went under but not many. The other night I traced the places I have been to in France & find I have been right from one end to the other along the coast & right across & over the Belgium border. Not a bad trip is it? I hope before long it will be the German boarder we cross & then get a range on to Berlin. It would be more satisfaction to knock down German villages than French. But never mind I expect we will be there all in good time.

You ought to see my dug out. Three of us have filled sand bags & built up a fine little show nearly as good as the old pig sty that I lived in for a month. I found a bed that some bosch left behind when the boys hunted them out so I can tell you when there is time to be in it we are comfortable. We have a hun helmet stuck up in front & old shells round the sides for fancy work so you see for the present we are sure of a shanty. . .

Well Dad both yours & Mum's birthday are due now and I want you to have something from me & as I can't send anything worth while from here I want you to spend my next pay & get what ever you like with it & remember I wish you both a happy birthday so try & make it one won't you. I wrote to you all a few days back & told Mum the same so do get something or I will feel hurt.

Tat Ta for the present & keep smiling with me

	I Remain
Give the	Your Loving Son
nipps my love	John

It was not until 20 September that Jack told his family about some of the horrors of that Somme offensive, including his first experience of a German poison gas attack:

Dear Mother Dad Sis & Bro

. . . I suppose dear all you have been wondering where and what we have been doing since coming into action . . . Well on the Somme we were in the open for 20 days & I will never forget those last 4 or 5 days we were there.

The aircraft spotted us & one night Fritz opened up on us with his heavy guns. Our Sergeant and 2 others were killed and 5 wounded. I think I told you before what hapened to me when I was sent on a message for more ammunition on a bike. Of course they took us out of that position & after a weeks spell we went in again a bit to the right of the other place. It was hot there too but we only lost 2 men.

The gas was the worst of the lot not that we cared about being hurt with it for our helmets keep it out but it was having to stay awake all the time for you can't sleep in the gas helmets.

The divisions time was up then for a change so we came out & had another weeks spell. I can tell you dears I was glad to be away so as to have a good nights sleep. When our spell was over of course we had to get to action again but this time we came up near Ypres & that is where we are at present. It is like having a holiday too after the Somme.

Over there the unburreyed dead were everywhere & there was no time to burry them. One day the water carts were being filled about a hundred yds down from the battery. Fritz must have seen them for he put a 5 point 9 right in the centre of them. You should have seen the mix up there was. No men were hit as it happened but two horses suffered. I saw a team and an ambulance blown to pieces another time & one night a team coming along the road was blown up by one of the horses kicking a hand bomb.

You see I have seen some sights that will never let me forget the war. I have always managed to get out of all the tight corners that I have been in so I think I must be like the cat have nine chances.

There was 4 of us filling sand bags when we came up here first & the ground was very hard in the place we were told to dig from so out we went into an open patch & started filling from a shell hole that was made about an hour before. We had just got a go on & Fritz caught sight of us & over came three 'whis bangs' [small shrapnel shells]. They fell short so you can guess we did not give him a chance to correct himself for we were contented to dig in the hard place after that. We watched a dual betwen 2 of our plaines & 3 taubes [German fighter planes] one day & they had been going like hammer & tongs for about 5 minutes when one of the taubes turned turtle & fell in flames. The other two pulled out then & started back but only one arrived back the other fell in no mans land full of holes. The one on fire fell well back in our lines & didn't we cheer our own machines.

Well dear all that is just about my doings up to date so you see I have seen a little bit of what war is. Out of this mail I got 9 letters & another from you dated 29 July. I am not doing to bad for letters 'Am I?' I am glad you got my photos allright. I think I will send over for the boy [brother Tommy] as a bomb thrower. Fancy him filling young Jacky Hallidy's eye up. Dad is quite right in saying he is the limit . . .

I got the little bunch of violets & I hope next time they are out I will be home picking a button hole for myself. I don't think it will last long now for the huns are being banged about every where. I think this is about all I can write this time so Tat Ta till next week.

Best of Love

I Remain

Your Loving Son & Bro Jack

XXXXXXXXX

A hindsight account of the Somme offensive is given in Jack's Postscript:

The guns were taken forward on the night of the 21st July. Next morning I was to see the effect of war as it really was. Here there were no green fields or apple orchards. Heavy fighting had taken place in this sector during the few days previous, in fact the Tommies had advanced pushing the Germans back & here we were with the guns in the old German 2nd line. Great shells had torn huge holes in the chalky soil & close by was a mine crater which had been fired a few days previously. Hundreds of unburied Tommies & German dead lay twisted & torn amidst the wreckage caused by the mine & the bombardment of both armies.

The din of battle was in the air. Eighteen pounder guns were almost wheel to wheel. Three lines of them. We were in the back line & behind us were sixty pounders & behind them nine point two's & further back heavier guns still. French 75's cracked away on our right. German shells were bursting everywhere. On the left of the ridge that our guns were firing from ran 'sausage gully'. Through the centre of this gully was a track which led up to the front line. Australian Infantry were now holding the line & we were to cover them in an attack which was planned for the near future.

Close to our battery was an underground 'dug out' some 30 feet beneath the surface. The Germans had sunk these shell proof quarters for their troops so we gunners made use of them when the shelling was heavy & we were not working on the guns.

Reserve ammunition was stacked by the guns & on Sunday 23rd July before daylight zero hour arrived for what was to be Australia's first major action in Flanders. At a given signal guns of all calibre crashed & flashed & hundreds of shells that were to pave the way for the advance of the infantry shrieked & roared through the chill morning air. From the gun positions we could see the glow of the bursting shells & rockets & flares soared upward from the German trenches. It seemed impossible that anything would remain alive in that hell of flame & flying metal. We were firing shrapnel shells & my time was fully occupied setting fuzes & passing the shells on to the loader.

The noise was terrific. From time to time lumps of dirt & chalk showered down on the gun crew & we knew we were under fire from the German batteries & at any time we could expect to be blown out. All day the bombardment was kept up & by the constant orders to increase range knew that our infantry were going forward. During the afternoon the rate of fire eased & I was for the first time in action ordered into the layers seat & there twirled the dial sight & set the bubble on the sight clino & pulled the firing lever. How often had I done that at gun practice in Australia with empty guns, but now those guns were speeding death to perhaps many. But it was war & the roar & crash as a German shell landed close quelled any qualms I may have felt at trying to kill men I could not see. They were trying to kill me & had killed some of my battery mates.

Wounded infantry were walking back, many of them driving small batches of German prisoners before them, terrified humans who looked as though they had glimpsed hell. They were safe now except those who happened to be caught by their own shell fire. This often happened and many of those walking wounded succumbed to those same shells.

Horse drawn ambulances slowly made their way along sausage gully bringing out the wounded that were unable to walk. Sometimes a shell would burst on the track close to those ambulances & often a whole team & party would be torn to pieces by the tearing flash of a bursting shell. Strange as it may sound but I did not at that period fear for my own safety. It seemed that one must go on playing the game & anyhow one stood as good a chance as the next. I think I was more bewildered than scared.

It was not till Wednesday 25th that the shelling on both sides eased down. Two factors caused this easing up. Our objectives had been reached & Pozieres had fallen to the Australian troops & they were consolidating the position. On the other hand the enemy was probably moving his batteries further back. We welcomed the spell & nerves were given a chance to calm down a little.

During the couple of days lull both the enemy & our aircraft were very busy. Constantly 3 blasts of a whistle warned those in the vicinity that a hun plane was overhead & everyone must stand fast. To move about & give the position away meant a shelling & as our guns were now out in the open we were not anxious to be picked up & registered on the target sheet of a hun 5 point 9 battery.

To date we had only lost one killed & he was unlucky enough to walk into a stray shell back in the quiet position up north. On the evening of the 27th our position was spotted & shell after shell crashed round the guns, covering everything with a thick layer of white dust but luckily he did not put any of our 22nd battery guns out of action & only wounded one of our men. Other batteries close by were not so lucky but we knew our time must come sometime.

Fighting planes met & fought above us & a cheer would ring out as a hun plane fell. A groan or a curse denoted that one of our planes had met the same fate. At this time Fritz seemed to be master of the air & although his planes were always met & engaged they got through & played havoc with our horse lines. Sometimes a hun plane would dive at us gunners & spray machine gun bullets about the position causing many quick dives for cover.

We came into a severe shelling during the evening of Aug 1st & the position was badly knocked about. My sergeant being killed with two other men. Several were wounded. It took hours to set the position in order again, but although some of the guns had been knocked about none were put right out of action.

Friday 4th Aug & the stage was set for another stunt. The Aussies were to take a ridge behind Pozieres & again we were to cover them. As before in the early hours of the morning the barrage opened & the boys followed the barrage to the German trenches & there fought it out & won the ridge & held it in spite of numerous counter attacks.

Jack's account of this savage action in a letter dated 8 August is a masterpiece of understatement, read in conjunction with his Postscript:

Dear Mother Dad Sis & Bro

Here we are again as well & bright as ever & hope you are all the same... Well dear all we are now out spelling for a while. I can tell you we are glad of a rest from the continual banging. Thank goodness we three got out of it alright except for a shaking up. According to the papers things ought soon to begin to look peaceful for I don't see how Fritz is going to hold out much longer. I suppose you have read all about our boys making more name in the latest stunts & they praise the artillery up too. We got a paper with it all in & you can bet we felt pleased for we were in the fun.

There is one thing next war I am going to be a big chap & tell them I can't ride a bike. As it is, every time anything was wanted from the waggon line John was given a bike & sent for it—the last night I went Fritz was shelling like one thing right over the hill I had to go. Well I got over allright & delivered the message & started back and then the fun started for I could see bursts between me & the battery & was wondering which track to take when one came close & sent dirt flying all over me. Of course I did not consider any way then just hopped on the jigger & trusted to luck & I had luck so the boys say for I got right up to our pits before the next came & it sent both me in & the bike into a trench with a bump. Of course I got a big scare and a shaking up but a good nights sleep made me feel the same old thing in the morning...

With best love and wishes mixed with kisses

                                    I remain
                                    Your loving Son & Bro
            XXXXXXXXXXXX   Jack

Thus Jack lightly brushed aside a bike ride that was to remain a nightmare to him until the day of his death. Twenty-five years later he recalled the terrors of it:

During our counter attacks the battery was running short of ammunition & I was called on to mount a cycle & ride for the waggon line with a message for shells. It was night & a night that will always remain a nightmare to me.

First as I followed a horse ambulance along sausage gully waiting for a chance to slip past, a shell roared down right under the poor devils who were on their way out to hospital. The sight almost turned my stomach & I lost my head for the moment & slinging the heavy bike across my shoulder started up the rise & was at once tangled in barb wire.

Somehow at last I reached the dressing station on the rise at La Boiselle & the road. Down the hill & through death gully which had been used by the Tommies as a cemetery, but as shells had since fallen in the gully it was more like a charnel house. As I tried to pick my way through the mangled remains & stay on the bike at the same time, a huge gun fired from the gully side & right over my head. I hadn't noticed the gun & my thoughts at the time concerned those poor devils I was riding over.

At the flash of the gun & the deafening roar in my ears I just collapsed in a heap but at once picked up myself & the bike & set off at a run up the other side of the gully & reaching the top was about to mount when another fellow coming along the track on a cycle crashed into me. Down we both went in a heap & both up in a moment & cursing each other set off in different directions.

I looked and felt more dead than alive by the time I had reached the waggon lines where the order for ammunition was handed over to the officer in charge. I must have looked like I felt as he offered me a nip of rum saying 'You look like you've been seeing ghosts.' So I had & war was getting no better faster. Aussie seemed a good place that night.

After half an hours spell I mounted the bike & reluctantly made my way towards where I knew those shells of the hun were bursting. From the hill at La Boiselle I watched the bursts of five nines well on our battery position.

The question was could I get back through the barrage in sausage gully & in one piece. Made a dash for it still riding the bike & reached the trench close to D sub gun. Only about 20 yards to go when with a roar & crash one landed.

The blinding flash was the last that I remembered till some hour or so afterwards & found myself at the bottom of the 20 foot dugout. By the faint light of candles I took stock of myself & wondered how I had got there & where was the bike. My eyebrows & lashes were singed & uniform scorched & inside felt like a jelly. Tried to stand & the old legs failed. That was a close one thought I wouldn't have had to be any closer.

It was the next day that I made a shaky trip up the steps into open air. The shelling had eased, but what a mess the position was in. Making my way to where I last remembered leaving the bike found a great hole in the trench side & the bike lying near. The open trench had taken the main force of the shell which must have landed almost under the bike.

From that night I was scared & for five nines held the deepest respect. On enquiry found that one of the boys had found me the previous night & dragged me into the dugout.

The battery went into action again at Mametz Wood that week and Jack recalled:

Mametz lives in my memory owing to the fact that the Scotties played their bag pipes & cheered as the guns rumbled past & as the sound of the pipes faded in the distance. Fritz greeted us with shrapnel & knocked out the A.M.C. orderly. Covered an attack made by the Jocks & Aussies & it was here that the friendship of the Aussies & Scotties became cemented for ever.

On the other hand, Jack did not appear to have a very good opinion of the Tommies (English soldiers), but he was not to understand the terrible battering those troops had received long before the Australians arrived on the scene.

France
26-8-16

Dear Dad

It is some time since I dropped you a line so am having a go at it now. How are things going now. I hope well for I am doing well. So far I have managed to stay in one piece & have a notion I will get through OK. I suppose in a day or so we will be among them again so I am making things hum while I can in the little town near here. The main thing is keeping the little mary well filled while my luck's in . . .

I see your note about the Tommies saying we put shells in their trenches but the fact is the Tommies are put right in the shade when our chaps go anywhere & all the girls take to us & leave them so they started a tale about us being no good.

But you ask any soldier (Aust) what our artillery is and they will all say the same. They are OK. Of course in the charges we often get some of our own for you just imagine trying to keep the shells bursting about 20 yds in front of them all the time. Some of the boys get ahead before we lift & they often blaim us for bad shooting but we keep lifting as they go ahead & I can tell you it keeps the boys going. We were praised by all the heads when it was over.

So you see the Tommies remarks are bosh. They haven't got over the hiding the boys gave their M.P.s when we first came to France & then pinching the girls turned them against us. Well Dad I will close up now & have a snooze so, so long for the present. Keep your end up.

P.S.   The sun has just come out,

so the rain might stop now for   I remain
a while   Your Loving Son
                                          Jack.

Gunner Duffell turned nineteen on 10 October but it was not the happiest of birthdays for our young hero, although the brigade was resting behind the lines at the time. He wrote home at the end of an eventful day:

In the field
10-10-16

Dear all at home

have just returned from a Christmas card buying expedition & have written them out to the different friends. I hope they will like them for they are the best I could get in this one eyed village here. Yes dears this is my birthday and I was just telling my mate about the difference between this & the last but all the same dears I am not minding it a bit but all the same by the next I hope to be back in Sunny N.S.W. Jack my hut mate & I invited another driver in to supper & we had some nice cocoa & salmon sandwiches quite a blow out we had.

I am kidding myself some man now you know but today at lunch time a great ugly useless moke lobed me in the ribs & sent me sprawling into a mud hole & I felt very small indeed when I got up. One of the chaps sang out (when he saw I was not hurt) 'There's a birthday box for you John'. As it happened I was too close to stop it properly.

There is a devel of a row going on over me too for in the stall I keep my horse in there are three others & the rotters started chewing the wood work so of course I thought I would stop them for I splathered tar all over the wood well this morning when we turned in to stables you should have just seen those 4 mokes. There was tar all over them. They tell me I will have to wash if off them with hot water but I can't see myself doing it somehow. This is with best love & I wish you all a Merry Christmas so try and make it one please

Night night from son Jack XXXXXXXXXXXXXXX

There was a happy ending to the day. Jack was excused from further duty by a considerate officer. While he was resting, the Australian mail came in with ten letters for Gunner W.J. Duffell and a big birthday parcel from his mother. 'After travelling 12 thousand miles to reach a man on the day it was meant for seemed a miracle,' he wrote.

6

Please Don't Mind the Mud

A week after Jack's birthday the brigade was suddenly moved to a place called Delville Wood in Flanders. Constant cold rain had made the horse lines a bog. The men were never out of wet clothes and the horses sank to their knees in mud. Jack described the fierce fighting that followed in his Postscript:

Delville Wood had been taken & retaken 3 times when we reached there & as no dead had been buried the sight was most gruesome. It was worst at night time when a man was on S.O.S. guard duty.

One seemed to be all alone with the dead & in the half light or dark they appeared to move if one kept his eyes fixed on one spot for any length of time. Anything will appear to move at night time & I remember firing my rifle into a stump one night. I could have sworn it was a hun bending over our telephone line which ran from the battery to the observation post, O.P. The incident took some living down, but as a gunner in another battery had walked out to speak to someone tinkering with the O.P. line a few nights before & instead of it being one of his own signallers mending the line it was a Fritz tapping the line for information & the gunner was shot down & the hun escaped. I was taking no risks.

There was very little rest in this position & no comfort at all. The shallow gun pits filled with water & dugouts oozed cold slimy mud & had a nasty habit of caving in & I have always had a horror of being buried alive. To make matters worse Fritz had the range to a yard & would open up on us anytime he liked.

The Delville Wood handicap as we called it was a daily occurrence as there was a trench by the edge of the wood & there the crews would rush when the shells began to fly. Of course if we happened to be firing ourselves it was just a matter of stay by the gun & take what was coming. A lot of the old cobbers went west about this position.

It was decided to move the guns into Flers closer to the front line. Positions had to be prepared so daily a couple of men from each gun crew had to go forward & in the face of constant shelling, try & fill sand bags with mud & build pits. As fast as we built the position Fritz would blow it to pieces. After a week of useless work it was recognised by the heads that Fritz would never allow men on guns in that position so the project was abandoned & we stayed in the old position & bad as it was we were pleased to know we would not be going to that hell on earth we had been ordered to prepare.

As the soldiers slogged away on the Somme, news reached them of the bitter conscription referendum campaign in Australia. Their reaction was mixed.

The referendum, held on 28 October 1916, had been called by the Commonwealth Labor Government led by W.M. (Billy) Hughes because voluntary system enlistments had declined. Australian casualties had been so high on the Somme that normal reinforcements and recruiting in Australia could not hope to fill the gaps in the five divisions in the field. Hughes maintained that the German threat to Australia and the Empire was so serious that an all-in effort had to be mounted. The referendum asked the people of Australia to authorise the call-up of all eligible unmarried men between the ages of twenty-one and thirty-five for military service.

In his book *The First AIF*, L.L. Robson describes the campaign as being marked by 'bitterness, conflict and confusion'. It was conducted in an atmosphere of patriotic fervour and violent emotions. The argument was exacerbated by the Irish Easter Rising and the execution of ringleaders by the British government. This led to bitter anti-British sentiment within men and women of Irish extraction in Australia.

The nation was split between Protestants and Roman Catholics and led to heated referendum meetings throughout Australia. Propaganda by both Yes and No proponents was hysterical and inflammatory. Whole families were rent over the emotive issue for a generation or more. The Labor Party and trade union movement feared that military conscription would lead to industrial conscription and the loss of other civil liberties.

Jack Duffell had vehement and angry views on the subject, though they were not shared by all his older mates. He looked with scorn and contempt on those who 'hadn't heard the bugle', as the saying went, or hadn't wanted to hear it.

What a lot of excitement the conscription business has caused over there. I think every one must be worrying over it except the ones it concerns most (the soldiers) & they don't care if the cold footed mob never come now for they will come in handy for the boys to keep their hands in when they get back. Anyway I have not lost any sleep over it except when the 5.9's were coming over pretty thick & then I would not mind changing places for a while.

He vent his feelings on some Hurstville neighbours in another letter:

Fred tells me E—— has a reject form saying he could not pass. I suppose the other low down cur has tried too (I don't think). Tell him there is some real good cold footed jobs going here if you crawl after them. He would be sure to get one of them for it would be hard to find a place for the likes of him in a fighting unit. By heavens it hurts to read of them hang backs when you see your cobbers going down & them having the good times at home. I reckon most of them had better get right away from the boys when they come home for they won't forget the scenes of those mad charges where men went down by the dozen & still they hang back. They ought to be rounded in like cattle & put in the front line & then the guns turned on them if they don't fight.

When the time came, Jack did not get a vote because he was not twenty-one, but he made known that it would have been a firm No. 'I reckon if the shirkers won't come on their own accord they are not worth bringing,' he said.

Conscription was defeated by the Australian people by a narrow margin. No votes totalled 1,160,033 to a Yes vote of 1,087, 557. There was surprise when the soldier vote favoured conscription by 72,399 votes to 58,894.

Not all who voted No did so because, like Jack Duffell, they did not want conscripts in their units. Others feared that conscription would mean the introduction of the hated death penalty for desertion, which was mandatory to the British Army. Under the Australian Defence Act, the death penalty was restricted to cases of mutiny and of desertion to the enemy. Official Australian war historian, C.E.W. Bean believed the most general motive for opposing conscription was not one without nobility. 'They themselves, when enlisted, had not known the trials and horrors of war,' he wrote. 'Now that they did know, they would not, by their own votes, force any other man into those trials against his will.'

Meanwhile in France, Jack continued to scribble his pencilled letters home under all circumstances, expressing constant concern over any family worries at Hurstville. In one letter he apologised for the mud on his letter:

Please don't
mind the mud

France
18-11-16

Dear Mother Dad Sis & Bro

This morning I received your welcome letter dated 17–9th & as I am not doing anything for a while will start an answer while I have a chance. At present I am at the guns doing our turn have been busy here for a week. I was sent for the day after I wrote the last letter. Fred went down for a spell and came up again yesterday. He is well & I believe still growing.

So poor Dad is not too well yet. I do hope Howe does him good. I can't see Dad leaving the pipe alone though. If he don't feel up to it he ought not to work too hard for a while & make use of the pay. I would rather you did that than work while sick. Well dears I am still OK myself but the mud is over the fence. Its Par Bon I can tell you. We have been issued with long boots but a chap sinks down that deep that very often it takes two or three to pull one out. But its all in the job so we put up with it as best as possible.

I see the friends are still keeping you company. Dad tells me you have bought a couple of talking birds. That ought to give the boy something to do teaching them. The only bird we see here is the starling and there are plenty of them. We heard this morning that conscription was beaten up to date also that Les Darcy has disappeared. We do get news you see.

Well dears this is only a short letter this time but perhaps I may be able to tell you more next time. Bye Bye for the time being & I hope you are all quite well by the time this reaches. Please remember me to the friends as usual. With best love & kisses to all.

I remain
Your loving Son & Bro
Jack

XXXXXXXXXXX

An early winter came to France and Flanders that year and weather conditions were atrocious during the late autumn of October and November. The first Battle of the Somme ground to another stalemate about the middle of November as the opposing sides dug in for the winter. Neither side had achieved much success. Haig's use of tanks for the first time on 15 September had surprised the enemy, but with only limited success.

The historian E.K.G. Sixsmith claimed that the Somme battle had certainly achieved two of its objectives. It had effectively drawn off German pressure on Verdun and the French army generally and it had prevented German diversion to other fronts. Sixsmith admitted, however, that what had been intended to be a decisive breakthrough had deteriorated into a battle of attrition. The fact was that, at great cost, the British forces had gained a strip of land about thirty-two kilometres long and ten kilometres deep, none of it of much strategic importance.

The Somme set in for what threatened to be an exceptionally cold and wet winter. And Jack was drafted to what he termed a 'soft job for the first time since he had left sunny old New South Wales'. Though loath to leave his battery mates, he was sent to a school of instruction for signalling. He also saw snow for the first time and wrote to his father about it: 'What do you think—we had some snow here the other day the first I have seen & I can't say I want to see any more either. It's a little too cool for this chick. The people here say it is "Bon" yet & I reckon its freezing so what will I do in the "Par Bon" weather?'

Jack was to see a great deal more snow before the year was out and there was not much he could do about it. Nonetheless, he spent a happy enough second Christmas away from Australia in 'a fairly large French town' (unnamed), although saddened by news of the death of the family's pet poodle, Trix:

France 26/12/16

Dear Mother Dad Sis & Bro,

At last I have got some mail but there was only one letter from you. The battery sent a lot of mail on to us they said but like everything else it's still coming. Any how I was ever so pleased to get one & to hear you were all well. Needless to say I am just the thing still. I also received 2 small parcels this morning. One from Netta the other from Vida Earl. I ought to get mail regular now for a while for the battery is out resting close by & I can always go down for mail.

Well dears Christmas is over & I had as good a time as anyone over this way I think. A few of us from the signalling school got leave to go to a fairly large town about 8 miles away & we stayed from Sat till Monday night. I had 40 francs so you see it was just enough to have a fair time on. We went to Service in the old church on Xmas morning but of course everything was carried out in French and although we understood little, it was very interesting.

Best of all though was our Xmas dinner & we had that in the 'Hotel-de-Paris'. It was about the best meal I have had since coming to France. The only bad part about it was there was no pudding. I don't think these people know what a pudding is & I got into a devil of a fix trying to explain. I wish I knew a bit more about the lingo.

I was sorry on reading Dads letter that poor old Trix had died. I could quite understand him dying of old age but Dad said something about he could not see if he had been shot. By heavens if I thought I knew of any one shooting him I reckon Id show them about as much mercy as the boys do the huns. But I don't think anyone would want to hurt poor old trix.

There are plenty of nice poodles etc over here. The women groom them up and cart them every where with them. In trains trams motors & every other blooming thing. Don't worry about the conscription business Mum. That mob of curs left there now are not worth worrying about but they had better get well away from the boys when they get back. I reckon I would rather risk a few of Fritz 5.9's than some of our infantry. They're the boys to fix up the sausage kings. Well dears I see Dad has got the garden in order again. I suppose it looks good now. Everything looks nice over here back a bit from the line but of course its bare up the front . . . Well dear all I will close up now for a week or so & I hope by then to have received all my other mail including parcels. I think the cold footed base mob get them.

Bye Bye for the present
      dears   I Remain
                                      Your Loving Son & Bro
                                      Jack XXXXXX

Gunner Duffell saw in the New Year of 1917 hunting chats on his body by candlelight until his concentration was interrupted by the sound of church bells ringing in a nearby French village and the shouts of his fellow soldiers:

Dear Mother Dad Sis & Bro.

Yesterday I received a heap of letters & Post cards & best of all 2 from home so I am setting too again to answer them. Although there is still a lot of back mail & parcels to come to go on with. These last 2 were dated 5th & 12th of Nov. so you see they are the latest. I see you are all well again & I can assure you dears that is about the only thing that I worry at all about, but now that I know that Dad is on the go again & you are all well everyting is OK. Except for the usual winter complaint (chilblains) I am 'good oh' so please don't worry about me for you may rest assured that this kid will get through allright . . .

Well I am glad you got the cards I sent from Belgium also hanky as Lil calls it. I thought it would take her eye. I see you have been getting some of our rain over there. I thought it must have gone over that way for it stopped raining here for a couple of days & on one of those the sun actually shone for about 3 hours. I guess by all accounts about the heat over there you would like some more of it.

I was sorry to hear about Edie Hornsby's husband being killed. Its hard on the poor girl but I suppose she feels the same about as many more young wives. I did not know that Perce Fletcher has stopped some of Frits medicine but if he is in England Ill bet he is glad of it. I wouldent mind getting one in a soft place myself to get over there for a while. So a couple more of the cousins have sailed eh? I'm hanged if I know what they want conscription for. Our lot ought to be able to make a mess of the Kaiser's push on our pats.

Well dears I saw the old year out & the new one in. But you will be amused when I tell you how.

I went to bed about 8 o'clock & one of the chaps said 'Arent you going to stay up for the New Year'? I said hang the new year & a few other remarks & went to sleep. But my 'boarders' kept waking me up, so after trying to get to sleep for 2 or 3 hours or more I said a few unprintable things about chats in general & pulled off my shirt, lit a candle & started hunting. All of a sudden the church bells started ringing & the boys singing out. So thats how I saw the year in after all.

This afternoon I am answering my 12 letters so I will come to a close dears so please remember me to all friends & relations especially Aunt Mary & I hope she is quite well long before this. Bye Bye for the present & with best love to you all

I Remain
Your Loving Son & Bro
XXXXXXXXXXXX Jack

Jack expressed deep indignation over another example of German frightfulness in his letter home of 14 January. He had been advised by a Sydney woman that her Christmas parcel to him had gone down with the liner *Arabia*, sunk by a German submarine. 'I expect a lot more of my mail went down with it,' he wrote. 'Thats another one up against Fritz he is making it too willing now sinking a chaps mail.'

The letter also expressed some alarm at the growing tenderness in letters from one of his ten girl correspondents:

France
14-1-17

Dear Mother Dad Sis & Bro

It is letter time again so I am setting too again to let you know that I am still going strong. I am back with the Battery again & I can assure you it goes against the grain turning out in the mornings for stables. You see we are out resting at present so all hands have to mess about with the horses. The weather is still trying to beat the North pole climate. Snowed all last night & half the day. You should have seen it flying about. It was worth a V.C. to walk out in front of the mob.

Well dear all I am expecting leave before very long & I will need some money in England so I cabled for £10 & hope you had it to spare at the time. I did not want to cable but you know a chap cant save anything out of a bob a day in this country for though the tucker issue is not bad, its not enough for this chic so most of my money goes to the canteen. I want to buy some warm winter gear when I get over the other side & I suppose it will be about the only chance I'll get to have a good time that is why I asked for the tenner.

Well dear Mum you seem to be terrible anxious about me keeping dry & warm but although I keep as dry as possible I often have a smile when I think of how you used to see that my boots were dry & keep dry clothes. Why my old 'clod-hoppers' have not been dry for a month or more & I have never felt any the worse for it.

I have a good scheme working now though for in this village there is a kind old French woman who cooks supper every night after we turn out of stables round we go to 'our' Madam & stay there by the fire till bed time. I take a dry pair of sox with me & dry the wet ones. So you see I always have dry sox in the mornings. Good home what? Hope we always come to this village to rest.

Yes dears I have had another parcel from you it was the one with the insecterside in. Thanks so much for it I think it hunted them out for a bit. The big parcel has not turned up yet worse luck or the one from England either Bob told me it had been sent over. I had a letter from Mrs Andrew Syd. saying that her parcel to me went down in the 'Arabia' I expect a lot more of my mail went with it. Thats another one up against Fritz he is making it too willing now sinking a chaps mail.

By jingo Jessie has been sending me some very serious letters this last few weeks. She seems to think she is the only apple on the tree.

I dont mind writing as a friend but she has gone over the line. I am afraid there will be some fun somewhere before long. I think its just as well that I am at the war.

Well I think I will have to close up now dear all till next week. I am at 'Our Madams' place now & am just about to swamp another coffee the fourth so far as well as some steak & chips. Doing well for a soldier don't you think? Good night dear all & please remember me to all the friends & share my best love & wishes between you

Bye Bye from Jack

XX XX XX XX

7

'Every Blooming Thing Is Frozen Stiff'

During the winter of 1916–17 both the Allies and the Germans battled against mud, rain and frostbite. Thousands of duckboards were laid on long tracks across the morass of the battlefields. Then from mid-January 1917, four weeks of colder brighter weather froze the land and water hard and covered northern France with snow. C.E.W. Bean commented:

The clogging of attack after attack in the mud of the Somme had now convinced Haig that all his troops could do for the remainder of the winter was, as far as possible, to keep up the strain on the Germans by means of small attacks and raids.

The Allies could afford the appalling losses better than their opponents. In the terrible determination with which Haig wore his enemy down the Germans really faced the beginning of the end.

Gunner Duffell summed it all up in a long letter home in late January:

France
25th Jan 1917

Dear Mother Dad Sis & Bro.

Just another few lines in answer to your ever welcome letter dated 2.12.16. You were all quite well then & I do hope you are the same when this reaches you. I am quite well dear all but you are not quite contented at my word I think. The cold weather has played its usual tricks on me of course, but other wise I am just the thing so please *don't worry.* I reckon I am doing well considering the difference in this winter & ours (Aust. I mean) for it has been ten deg below freezing point for about a week & for about two months it has never been much above 30 The snow has almost turned into ice & every blooming thing is frozen stiff.

Of course I do my fair whack of grumbling especially when the boots are frozen in the mornings but that is the soldiers privilige they say. You say most of the letters you see are full of the hard times we have. Well dears I could do the same I suppose but hang it all its all in the game & I dont see the use of crying out about it. Some chaps must have expected it to be a soft job all the time.

What do you think? We have shifted from 'Our Madames' village. I assure you it goes against the grain a bit not having the warm kitchen to go to for supper. I hope we go to a good position next time in action where we can have a fire. By all accounts the strike has been shaking things up a bit over that way. I suppose you are not sorry to see the end of it.

Its a funny life this for one never knows how long they will be in one place but I know one thing & that is that we will be well in the thick of it in a day or two. I cant grumble though for I've had a long spell out. Well all the weather is still about the same. Yesterday there was 15 deg of frost. That beats Aust. winter 'what'? Its got my feet tickled up though for I had to to see the quack this morning & get one dressed up a bit. I'm getting a bit of a cold too but I don't think it will be much. What do you think? Things have been mixed up again & half our Battery have been put in another battery & it has altered the leave list. I was due to go any time but now goodness knows when my turn will come. Rotten luck dont you think. I will put the money by when it comes so it will be all the same in that respect.

Fred and & I are still together in fact all of us from the other battery are. I don't know where Bob's lot went to but it wont take long to find them when we get into action. Fred is well but going pop about the weather like every one else.

I had the luck to strike a few nights back a chap who was broke & trying to sell a bonzer pair of leather gloves lined with fur so I got to busness with him & finished up by getting the gloves for 5 francs. They must have cost about ten bob new so I did well 'eh?' There some swank & warm too.

At present I am doing a guard in the old gun pit well up in the line again. Its five a/m & I have been up since a little after three. I have a good old fire going in an oil drum so the cold does not get much of a say. I assure. At six I will call Fred up to have a turn for you see someone has to be up and awake in the pit all the time. The feet are still a bit sore & the cold has not gone away yet but it will have a chance to get well now I think.

I hope your parcel with the custard & milk comes along very soon for I guess I would make some grand old feeds for the detachment. I am trying to get some eatables sent up from a canteen so if everything arrives we will be right there on the pig's back. 'Oh gee whis' the wood has run out. I'll have to go out poking about in the blooming snow for more. Fred won't say a word if the fire is out when he comes on.

Well now dear all how is everything doing over that side? Have those smart police strung up the I W W mob yet? If they came out here & started burning places down I could understand it for I would not blaim anyone for trying to keep warm. By the sound of things I think someone must be throwing fire-works about out side. I don't suppose its one of Fritzs pet 5.9s by any chance. 'Oh no.'

How is Dad getting on with the garden. I wouldent advise him to send the boy round selling things for by all accounts of him I think sweet shops would see a lot more of the hard cash than you would. Thank Lil for her little letter. As you say she is a bad writer, but I cant talk. I guess my fingers are more at home on a bridle or pick or shovell than on a pencil . . .

Well dears its time to close up now so I will ring off & get some wood. Remember me as per. to all the friends & keep my best love and kisses yourselves.

Bye Bye for the present

PS	I Remain
Don't get caught in the	Your Ever Loving Son & Bro
wire entanglements	XXXXXXXXXXXXXXXXXXXXXXXX Jack
	XXXXXXXXXXXXXXXXXXXXXXX

The icy cold and rain was still the main topic in a letter a few weeks later:

France
8/2/17

Dear Mother Dad Sis & Bro.

another letter letting you know that I am still pluging along in the great war & can't make any complaints only something has gone wrong with the weather clark. He still refuses to raise the temperature more than 20 degrees.

I am in the same position as when I wrote the last letter & hope we will stay here for some time for it's not a bad corner & we always have a good old fire going in the pit. Its a bit over the odds though when it comes to getting water in a sand bag to get a mug of tea for that's what it ammounts to now. It tickled me when I got the first lot of water & had to take a hammer to break the ice up small enough to put in a sand bag.

Well dear all I received two more of your ever looked for letters a couple of nights back also the photo of the Little Grey Home & wasn't I pleased to get it. You all look well I am glad to say. By jove, the boy has grown. I can see he will be running the show soon. The bangalow has grown some too.

My mail also had a letter from the bank in London telling me that my money was there & they wanted to know if I wanted it sent over, but I will write back & tell them to keep it there for me. It's a bit rotten you know, getting split up just when we did for it has made a terrible hash of the leave list. I would have been enjoying my ten days furlough now if things had gone on in the usual way. I don't know how long it will be before my turn comes. . .

Love & Kisses to all
from Son & Bro
Jack XXXXXX

While workers in Australia were on strike for more pay, the soldier boys were doing their best on a few shillings a day. Jack confessed to some financial worries in a letter at the end of March:

France
27-3-17

Dear Mother Dad Sis & Bro.

its letter time again but I don't know how I am going to compose one with no news. I have not had any mail since writing last but there is a mail expected any time now. Well dear all I am still going strong except for sore feet (which don't count). The weather has changed completly & it is cold as ever again. Raining & snowing in turn nearly every day. According to the Frenchies it should be nice weather now. . .

Our pay books were ballanced the other day and anyone overdrawn has to reduce their pay till it squares up again. Of course WJD was overdrawn to the extent of £5 so for the next couple of months I will draw the large sum of two bob a week.

I suppose you will wonder how I came to be that much out but I assure you dear all one bob a day is not enough to keep a chap going

On Active Service

 WITH THE BRITISH EXPEDITIONARY FORCE

No 2.

Address Reply to :

Gnr W J D
Knocking spots off
Germans in every direction

Frogland 25 May 1916.

My Dear Dad.

Here I am again having another go at the letter writing buisness. (I'll soon be some class at it) How are you? I hope you can say just the thing. How am I? well I am as well as can be & feeling quite jolley. I don't know why though unless its the prospect of staying up till 12 oclock to cart huns death warrants about. I am not having a bad time you know I feel pretty happy sailing along with me little tin hat on the side whistling all the old songs I can think off. There's plenty of dodging to be done for on the way to one of the joints I have to go to most of the houses have taken it into their heads to spread all over the roads (I wonder why that is) I was thinking of asking the huns to oblige me by dropping their shells on the paddocks instead of the middle of the road for it causes such a lot of cuss words to flow when a fellow drops into them of a dark night. We had some fun here

Portion of the letter transcribed on pages 39 and 40 (it continues on the following page)

(2)

last m night. Just after tea two other chaps &
I were playing with one of the mascots when over
comes a "whiz & a bang just outside the billet. Needless to say we were soon there too. Just as well for
over came 2 more & one went through & open
door & burst in the stable. The old French johney
who owns this ranch had his only cow tied up
there & the poor beggar stopped about a pound
lumps of shell case behind the right lug. The
Vet stitched her up but I don't think she will
get over it. Well about us now About 5 or six
of us made for the dug outs for they were putting
them in rather fast & we thought they were
going to put our billet down south. The scrap
lasted about 20 minutes & when they knocked
off you could see heads sticking up out of every
hole in the place looking for the rest. Thank
goodness noone noone was hurt & the billet was
not hurt much for only the one hit it I think
They started putting them into a little village
about 1000 yds. from here then & we stood & watched
the the mess they made of it. Of course it was
deserted long ago & shelled before also
but we could see the places going all directions
One shell put in the right place means one house
in the wrong place. Its some experience you

Its getting too dark to write any more so I'll have to close. Escaped pencil but I lost everything except my pocket book & Bible from the church. The belt of badges, money belt, pen & lots of little things I wanted to take back. Best of love to you all from son & Bro. Jack xxxx

Weymouth
England
17·7·18

Dear Mother Dad Sis & Bro.

about the time this reaches you I should have arrived back, but Fritz hadn't finished with the boy so I'm back in England again. Made a start on Sunday the 14th went 360 miles or so when up popped a sub & jammed a torpedo into our old tosh. He missed the engine room as luck would have it & tore half our starboard side away between the engine room & bow. Great joke (don't think) jumping into the adlantic ocean. but it had to be did. We had four nurses & some bad chaps aboard & of course they were swung out in the boats, but the rest of us had to take to the water & be picked up by the boats after the destroyers had taken the nurses etc. aboard. We were all taken on destroyers after Fritz had been fired up & sailed back to old Blighty at 27 notts. Our ship was one of the hun boats captured from the outbreak of war, but it

Portion of the letter describing the loss of the *Barunga (pages 135–6). It
continues on the following page*

2

was her first & last attempt as a troop ship.
I hear we are the first load of returning
"Aussies" to be torpedoed, but now its all
over I wouldn't have missed it for quids.
Everyone keep cool & as far as I can hear
no lives were lost. The boys went over
in good orders a few at a time. The navy
swell prevented the life boats coming
alongside so we had to swim out. Many
took to the rafts & waited till everyone
came from the ship & then they struck
out for the destroyers. You could see about
half a dozen on a raft hanging on & singing
or cracking jokes at the swimmers etc. One
mob were singing "This is the end of a
perfect day." It was about 5 in the evening
so they were about right. We got into
dry stuff about 2 hours after being struck
& you should have seen us coming off
in our dry clobber, some in sailors rig
others in Tommy & several with civvy
stuff. I managed to grab a pair of long
pants, a pair of canvas shoes & a shirt.
I hung to my tunic & dried it as I went
along. Have all Aussie stuff again
now though as they fitted us up this afternoon.
We came back to our own camp
& expect to have another try in a few weeks
time

over here. Even one orange costs 2½ francs & cakes half the size of our penny cakes cost the same. So you see it does not take long to spend seven shillings at that rate.

Most of the lads draw two shillings a day & it's all they can do to make it spin out when buying a little extra in the eating line.

When the summer starts it will be easier to do on one bob for a chap wont want so much to eat. Just imagine a deacent feed of eggs when they cost fourpence each but they are about all we can get most of the time so we have to have them . . .

We got payed this afternoon so of course J & I have just returned from the 'eat up joint'. I was payed the large amount of 10 francs so J will have to do most of the paying during the next 2 weeks for two feeds will finish my little lot. Fred is in some where the same state too. We are in hopes of getting leave together during next week to a decent town & will have our photos taken if possible. Well now dear all I will close up for the time being so give the nips my best love & a kiss each also a large share of both for you & Dad. Remember me to all the friends as per usual.

Bye Bye for the present dears\
from Son & Bro\
JackXXXXXXXXXXXX

Jack Duffell never forgot that terrible winter of 1916–17, and twenty-five years later he recalled the misery and peril of it:

Everything was frozen by this time, the pools were ice covered 9 inches thick. Frost cogs were fitted to the horse shoes otherwise no horse would stand on the ice covered roads. Snow 2 feet deep covered the land & a stiff wind blowing off this seemed to go clean through sheep skin vests. I put on all the clothes I possessed & was still frozen until it was painful to breathe.

As the column moved from Rainville to Behencourt, Gunners took turns at relieving the drivers to enable them to walk & warm up a little. My feet were so bad that I reported to the Brigade Medical Officer who put me off duty for the rest of the day. Although wearing gum boots 3 sizes larger than I normaly wore my feet would not fit into them & it was agony to walk about.

The war was still raging though & we were on our way back into it. We were to relieve at Highwood. Sunday 28th Jan the guns were left at the waggon lines & the gunners made to the positions & took over the guns that were already in covered pits. This seemed a much better idea than pulling one lot of guns out & the relieving crowd having to drag their guns in & fit up the dismantled position. Except for a few raids, Infantry action was at a standstill, owing to the thick covering of snow. Anything that was not white showed up in the snow & we were hard put to keep the position as natural as possible & so escape the inevitable shelling that would follow once we were spotted.

After every shoot we would shovel snow back over the black patches that were caused by the blast from the gun muzzles. The six black bare patches that appeared in front of the pits would be spotted by the first enemy plane flying over & then five nines to follow.

Thick fogs set in while in this position & during these fogs we were compelled to fire on only registered targets such as cross roads etc as the results of the shooting could not be observed. We had fires going in the pits during those times & did lots of jobs in the open, knowing that Fritz observers could not spot us either. These fogs came down very quickly & at any time during day or night. At one time I was on the way to the O.P. when one came down & I wandered about for a couple of hours. My chief concern was that I might stray in front of a gun position which might open fire. I made my way towards one battery that had opened up & to my delight found it my own. I had turned round in the fog & was not sent out again on the O.P. job till the fog cleared.

The water in the shell holes had frozen & ice was a foot thick. This ice had to serve as drinking water when melted down. It was impossible to carry water from the waggon lines to the guns as it turned to ice long before it reached the guns. Sauce & all tinned stuff was frozen hard & had to be broken instead of being poured from the tins. If warm water were used for washing it had to be dried off quickly or would freeze on the skin. I have combed fine ice from my hair after wetting it before combing. Yes it sounds tall but it's true.

Then the thaw set in & soon the landscape changed from spotless white to one of slush & icy cold mud. The shell holes were now full of water & mud, the ice having melted. We made a distressing discovery when one of the boys went to the shell hole we had been getting our water from for the past month. Lying at the bottom of the hole was a well & truly dead Fritz. The ice had hidden him up till now.

We were given more to think about than dead huns, though. The live ones had prepared good strong positions some ten miles behind the line they held during the Winter & just before the thaw set in they quietly withdrew to those strong positions leaving a sea of mud & open country that we must negotiate before making contact again. Orders were issued to the Artillery to move forward & range on the enemy. This was easier said than done.

All night we toiled in that sea of mud & shell holes. As many as 20 horses were hooked onto a gun & after capsizing 2 guns into deep shell holes we realised what a hopeless task had been set us. 'Get them out & come into action from our old front line, the infantry had gone forward & are depending on us' said the Major. So we had another go.

It was pitch black night & cold as sin, everyone was wet to the skin but sweat trickled down my face as I strained & pulled on the drag ropes. A rope parted & half a dozen of us measured our lengths in the churned up mud.

By morning four guns were out & on a bit of firm track in the rear of High Wood. One driver was missing. He had been somewhere in the centre of a 20 horse team but somewhere during that mad scramble he had been jerked out of the saddle & we knew what had happened to him. Trodden into the mud by the horses following. Someone was ordered into the empty saddle. The guns must go forward. They did go forward finally per medium of a light railway & trails were bedded down just in front of the trench our boys had occupied & held during that dreadful winter.

Then Fritz came over in force. It appeard that the Australians were following too close on his heels so this attack was meant to drive us back Fritz was met with bomb & bayonet & suffered a crushing defeat. Truck load after truck load of bayoneted & wounded prisoners were taken back after that mornings work. The wounded huns received the same good treatment that was afforded our own men.

The brigade was relieved at 2 a.m. on 6 March, the men and horses having been in action throughout the winter. Jack records that he undressed that night and 'slept like a log'. Next day he had his first bath, except for icy shell-hole dips, for a couple of months. The brigade rested and refitted at Behencourt for four weeks, although the 'rest' proved to be a misnomer. Jack reported that the men 'worked like niggers in mud and slush every day attending to the horses and guns, so everyone was glad when the orders came to get back into action again'.

8

The Hot Guns of Bullecourt

The spring had come to France and Flanders and with it good and bad news for the Allies. The Czarist government of Russia fell in a sudden revolution on 8-9 March, to be out of the war by December. On the other hand, the United States declared war on Germany in April, with a million troops landed in France within a year.

'Everything that is not smashed up is getting green again,' Jack reported. 'You could never imagine how high the spirits of the boys has risen. Although even when the mud was at its worst, the boys still kept a smile and a joke going.'

There was still no news about Jack's Blighty leave although he had been in the front line, with only local leave, for nearly a year. Signs of some war weariness were evident in his still cheerful 'keep your pecker up' letters. 'I have not heard any more about my Blighty leave,' he wrote, 'but I reckon its time they came to light with my pass. I want to have a look at this wonderful Blighty & incidentally get well away from the blinking war for a while.'

During the 'rest' period at Behencourt, however, Jack found time to ponder over the exploits of his young brother in Hurstville with a sense of shocked pride and amused awe. His name was Harold but for some reason unknown to the Duffell family now, Jack called him Tommy and Tommy called him Jacka. Now about three or four years old, Tommy was apparently terrorising his parents and the neighbours' children, as passages from Jack's letters over a period of about a year reveal:

I say the boy must be getting some Kid, Fancy him telling you to shut up when you tried to sing him to sleep. I am thinking he will be getting a little stick after him soon . . .

Fancy Tommy getting round with his guns shooting turks for Jacka. Tell him to pot off germans instead. But he neednt of closed that next door kid's eye the way he did . . .

I'll let you look after the Kid though for what a young devel he must be getting. He will break his young neck if you don't watch him but I think the best thing you can do with him is put a uniform on him & send im over to me to amuse the mob . . .

By Gee I would like to see the boy. What a young dooer he must be. Fancy him outing that kid with a paling. I reckon they want a few like him on the front line when Fritz comes over. I can see myself taking a back seat if he gets much stronger.

These reflections about the juvenile terror campaign being conducted in far-off Hurstville ended abruptly on Good Friday, 6 April, when the brigade was on the move again, warned that heavy fighting was awaiting them. The weather had changed and snow fell during the night.

There had been dramatic developments at the front during their absence. The Germans had retired to the Hindenburg Line during March. The British 3rd Army at Arras struck the first blow of the Allied great offensive planned for that year. The Australians had taken Bapaume after bloody fighting followed by the battle of Bullecourt where the Australian 4th Division seized for a time part of the Hindenburg Line.

Jack's letters are very sketchy about the brutal fighting to follow. One conjectures that for once he was too exhausted to write or that his letters were censored. His Postscript describes the action vividly:

All that day we travelled through the country just taken from Fritz. Both German and Australian dead were passed & in such numbers that showed how severe had been the fighting.

Bapaume that had been a fair sized town was reached by evening. It was just a brick heap. Fritz had blown the place to pieces before he evacuated. Roads were mined & as time fuzes had been left these mines went up any old time so we expected to go sky high any minute while making through that town.

The town hall, the only building left intact suddenly went up with a roar. Those inside or in the vicinity going up with it. Some German prisoners who were halted close by went up together with the guards.

Reaching the other side of this ill fated town we were surprised to find the country open & in good condition. Except for a stray shell hole or two it looked quite natural. There had not been any rear guard fighting here. Fritz had hurried over it & settled in his prepared positions about 5 miles further on.

We were putting the finishing touches on the pit & getting everything ready for the big stunt when on Sunday 15th Ap. like a bolt from the blue Fritz came at us.

Early in the morning with a mist to hide his advance our front line was over run & soon Fritz bullets were zipping about the gun positions. So fast & sudden had been the attack that no S.O.S. signal went up & the first the gun crews knew about it was when Fritz came on the positions with a rush.

We were helpless & guns useless as the huns were sticking to the sunken road & working round behind us. There was only one thing to do & we were ordered to take the breech blocks & sights & make for the waggon line. It was either that or be shot or bayonetted where we stood. As Fritz came on we retired to where reinforcing Infantry were coming up to stop Fritz's mad rush. We saw the 19th Battallion meet & engage Fritz & at once the hun turned but very few got back.

We again manned the guns & fired over our Infantry & into the gap the huns had advanced through. Everywhere huns were lying either shot or bayonetted. Some of our guns had been blown up but Fritz had got the worst of it & 1,500 of his picked troops were killed.

Gunner Duffell describes the savage battles of Bullecourt that followed. The battery directed its fire on the German barbed-wire entanglements and machine-gun positions. The Germans replied with heavy and accurate shelling, blowing out four of Jack's battery guns. Dozens of German planes flew over the battlefield and spectacular air fights were witnessed.

Jack was lucky to be 100 metres away from his usual gun when it received a direct hit. A piece of hot metal from its range drum landed at his feet and he kept it as a souvenir.

The Allied assault on Bullecourt began at 3 a.m., thousands of shells from hundreds of guns pounding the German positions as the infantry prepared to advance. At 6 a.m. Gunner Duffell was relieved after firing 300 rounds:

I was pulled from the layer's seat & a fresh man took over. I sat on the ground a deaf & shaking heap covered in oil as the guns had heated up & the oil squirted out at every recoil. It is a severe job to fire for 3 hours at the rate we had been sending them over. I was like a jelly & just sat with my face pressed into my oily, grimy hands, hearing & feeling nothing for over an hour.

Bullecourt was captured but the price had been high for both sides, with many Australian casualties. 'Hundreds of prisoners were brought back & they were so terror stricken that in many cases no armed guard was needed to urge them on,' wrote Jack:

I saw some batches of 25 or 30 following a wounded man with perhaps a couple of others bringing up the rear & armed only with a mills bomb or service pistol.

The weather had turned quite hot by this time & many of us had stripped to the waist. We looked a wild & woolly crew as we bogged into bully beef & army bread at 6 p.m. There had not been time for eating for the past 12 hours. A tot of rum before zero & another at cease fire. Two tots in one day—we knew we must be winning.

Gunner Duffell had another of his narrow escapes from death when the guns were being moved into a new position. The Germans spotted the movement of the horses and opened fire. 'As we moved off a shell splinter knocked my helmet off,' Jack wrote. 'I had often complained at having to wear that heavy steel helmet, but I took it all back when I saw the dent the splinter had made in the "tin hat". It had saved my brains being spread about the countryside.'

At last it was all over for a while and the brigade moved back forty kilometres to their quiet little village of Behencourt for a spell. True, German planes often flew over and bombed the horse lines, but that was merely a source of irritation to the battle-hardened troops. Everyone was inoculated again against typhoid:

That made about seven times I had taken the needle since I joined up. A man must have been full of dope but I expect that is about all that kept us alive in that hell of filth, disease & stench. Some wonderful feeds of eggs & chips or anything that was going was eaten. At one sitting I put away 18 eggs but that was a record, 6 eggs with chips & coffee was about the usual order.

The battery had a real rest this time at Behencourt, joining in divisional sports tournaments for boxing, running, football, horse racing and for the best gun teams. Jack spent most of his time reading and writing letters under shady trees. He also went swimming in a nearby creek. His letters do not specify the sort of books he read but in later life he was absorbed in anything relating to facts and figures, in a continual search for knowledge. On the lighter side he is known to have enjoyed the works of Nat Gould, a best-selling Australian author of horse-racing novels.

He wrote letters late into the twilight, such as this one to his mother:
'At present I am writing under a bonzer tree out in a field & it is
somewhat about 8 oclock but still light & will be until about 9.30 p.m.
I am not having so many eggs this time out for the simple reason that
the cash won't stand it but never mind I'll make up for lost time in
Blighty.'

Jack's devotion to his father and mother was quite touching and he
wrote private letters to his father when he wished to discuss personal
matters which might worry his mother:

France
17-6-17

Dear old Dad

I was glad to get your usual letter this morning & am writing a few
lines all to yourself again. Was glad to hear that you were doing pretty
well again Dad. I was anxious for a while when you were bad & I know
you always made it out to be light. You might as well tell me just how
things are going Dad for I can always tell by the tone of the letters.

I was nearly forgetting about your birthday this time, even now it will
be late but better late than never Dad so I wish you the best birthday
wish under the circs & to make things better I want you to spend what
you like out of next pay & buy yourself something that you want. Its
no use sending anything for over here Dad it would only reach the base.
I guess it is getting dark so I will have to shake it up.

Most of us are going in for open air treatment this weather & I assure
you its great. Today J P & I had two swims. We are often glad to drink
the same water but a chap cant do without a dip this weather. You would
not imagine how soft we are now. A 100 yds walk is quite enough to
bring the sweat out. During the winter we got as pink as Tommies but
now the good old brown is beginning to show up again. I suppose you
are getting it a bit colder over that side now. Hope the water dont freeze
while you wash like it did here. Don't get your water in a bag either. . .

Well Dad I will have to ring off till next mail so keep a stiff upper lip
& keep the Mater smiling.

Bye Bye
from Son
Jack

While at Behencourt, Jack took the whole family into his confidence
in expressing concern about the wisdom of safety in numbers and writing
to ten girls at the same time. At the ripe old age of nineteen, going on
twenty, he was beginning to find out about women:

In the field
22-6-17

Dear Mother Dad Sis & Bro,

. . . Dad says he is going to buy the house next door & get it ready for me and the little French bride but you need not have any fear of that. There is not going to be any French brides for John. The good old Ausy girls will do me I guess.

By the way I had a letter from Jessie the other day & got a devel of a shock for she was at Hurstville again. I did not expect her to turn up there or I would never have answered her letters. I guess I can see a bit of a mix up one of these days. Girls again. They are always getting a chap into trouble I wrote to Rhoda & squared myself in that quarter but I can forsee trouble ahead all the same. How is Mary Dircks getting on? She calls herself my cousin now so you see I am doing allright over there. I might get one out of the lot even now.

In another letter of the same period, he discussed the soldiers' view on heroes and heroism. In short, he preferred a pair of dry socks to his name on an honour board in Australia:

I wonder how many more honour boards want my name. If they keep going I will be kidding myself a bit of a hero I wonder if they know that the boys would be much more pleased if they spent the money on some smokes or something that would be some use over this way. I was yarning to an Infantry chap one day about the same thing & he says he has his name on about 20 different boards over in Australia but he said not one of the clubs etc have wondered if he was dying for a smoke or a pair of sox. He said its all very fine every one saying your a hero but he would much rather see the dinkum article.

A few days later Gunner Duffell got the dinkum article he was seeking. He was told to report to Albert railway station for his ten-day furlough in Blighty.

9

Blighty at Last

Blighty was a British Army slang word meaning England or home. It was applied to a wound or a furlough that secured a return to England, and the word was adopted by all English-speaking soldiers in World War I. To them it meant heaven, paradise, nirvana, Xanadu—take your pick—after the horrors of France. Some soldiers shot themselves in the foot to get a Blighty. The word's origin is obscure, though it is thought to have been coined by British troops in India from an Urdu word pronounced bildti, meaning European or foreign.

Jack Duffell had despaired of ever getting his Blighty, but when it came he was determined to enjoy it to the full. This he did for ten wonderful days. Mind you, he would have much preferred Hurstville but that heaven was unattainable at the moment.

He chummed up with another Blighty man, Jack Harris, a gunner of his own age in another battery who had also left Australia in the troopship *Berrima*. The pair entrained at Albert railway station on the Somme for Boulogne and then across the English Channel to Folkstone and London. 'A man felt like a fish out of water but what a relief it was to be back in civilisation,' Jack Duffell wrote later:

Our first move was to obtain new underclothing and book into the Wilton Hotel.

A good soak in hot water & to bed for a sound & certain undisturbed sleep in a real bed with sheets & an eiderdown quilt. I expected to wake & find it all a wonderful dream.

I think the best part of that leave was the feeling on awaking next morning. There was no reveille & I did not have a watch. Wasn't it wonderful to be in that soft bed & know that it didn't matter. I could get up when I liked order the breakfast I liked most & as much as I wanted.

While I lay wondering what the boys were doing, Big Ben of London chimed out the hour of 8. A soft tap on the door by a porter, he asked if I'd take a cup of coffee & have a paper. Too right I would.

Jack was occuping a single bed in the same room & as he was still asleep I threw my legging at him. He woke with a start & I yelled wake up! Battery action, S.O.S.! As the grin appeared on his dial I told him the gent in the frock coat wanted to know if he'd take a coffee & paper. We drank the coffee & read about the big war.

By nine o'clock we were dressed & presented ourselves for breakfast. Sugar & fresh milk on the porridge & bacon & eggs to follow. Paying for the night's lodging & breakfast we wandered out & hailed a taxi & were driven to the Bank of Australia where money I had cabled for was waiting. Jack had money there also & we emerged from the bank each richer by £15.

The first day was spent in seeing the sights of London, shopping & eating. Booking seats for the evening session at a Theatre we decided to book up a room at a quiet little house in Tennison St. Waterloo. It would seem more like home that a hotel. After partaking of the best dinner possible we took up our seats at the Theatre. High Jinks was the show & we enjoyed it immensely.

The two young Australians spent two days in London. Though not exactly painting the town red, they had a whale of a time, experiencing the sights and sounds of one of the world's great cities with wonderment and delight. One gets a picture of stocky little Gunner Duffell briskly absorbing everything with his dark observant eyes as prime material for his next batch of letters to Australia. 'You would not believe how nice it is to be away from the chats,' he wrote to his mother:

I have a hot bath every morning & have bought a pair of light Boots. I nearly broke my neck trying to walk about in the iron shod military boots on these footpaths. The first night on a soft bed was awful but next night it was better and now we have got used to them.

I am sending you a small parcel home containing a few little things and am enclosing my best love too. The piece of range drum is off D gun after Fritz had had a dirrect hit on it. The whole concern was smashed up & that is all that was left of the range drum. There is also a little Australia that I cut out of a hun water bottle at Pozieres & a shrapnel ball that smacked my steel hat one day. The belt of Badges I am sending home because I am tired of carrying it about.

Jack Harris invited 'Duff', as he called him, to accompany him to South Wales to visit an aunt and two girl cousins he had never met who lived at Skewen, a small town near Neath in Glamorganshire. The pair made their way there via train to Swansea and the Harris family at Skewen welcomed them with open arms. 'The old lady treated us like a Mother & my word the girls, Cassie & Beattie, were pretty & nice,' Jack told his family. 'Three wonderful days of real home life were spent with these fine people.'

They were the first Australian soldiers the town had ever seen and no doubt the two Jacks swanked around a bit in their Australian uniforms, with the distinctive slouch hat turned up on one side. (The hat was a favourite with English cartoonists, who theorised that it was turned up one side to assist unimpeded cheek-to-cheek encounters with pretty girls.)

'The girls were proud to walk out with us & of course we did not mind walking out with them,' Jack wrote. 'They wanted us to spend the whole of our leave with them but we wanted to look round England a bit before returning to the front. They made us promise that if we ever happened to stop a Blighty or get leave again we were to spend it at their place.'

The pair left Skewen for Blackpool, the working-class holiday fun capital on the Lancashire coast. They travelled by night 'so as to have the daylight for pleasure'. This involved a six-hour wait at Preston for a connecting train at 7.30 a.m. Guess how Jack spent those early morning hours on Preston railway station? He set to work in the waiting room catching up with his correspondence. The letter to 'Dear Mother Dad Sis & Bro' revealed two items that most certainly would have been blue-pencilled had he been back with the battery and subject to censorship:

What do you think the Gaur Dam Yanks said when they arrived in France? Some of our boys (Ausy) got talking to some of them at Le Havre & the Yanks said they guessed it was time we guys woke up (meaning the Ausyies) & they also said they would do as much in three months as we did in the same number of years.

Oh gee whis that ended the matter for our boys hopped right into them & I reckon if Fritz towels them up like they did, they are in for a bad time. I believe the military does not intend to put U.S.A. troops in with Australians.

There was trouble amongst our own mob some time back. You know during the Winter the 3rd Aust Division were kept in England. & the 1st 2nd 4th & 5th Divisions went through all the Somme business & when the weather got better the 3rd Anzacs were brought accross to take Messines after all the huns had been blown up by mines.

Well Fritz came at them one morning & cut them up a bit so the 4th Div. was sent up to give the dear little chaps a hand & bless your life if the 3rd didn't start slinging off at the 4th. They reckoned the 4th had been having a good time while they had to take Messines. Of course that started the bust up that ended in 10 deaths & 40 hurt. Fists are not used in those kind of arguements.

The boys have got hardened to anything now. I heard a couple of infantry talking about an Officer they captured, he turned up his nose & said he would only give himself up to an officer of equal rank. They told him that there was a war on & they had no time to look for officers so they pushed him down one of his own dugouts & threw a couple of bombs after him & then went on looking for loot. They reckon there is only one falt with the Russians they take too many alive.

Blackpool turned out to be all they had expected, and they made the most of it while their money lasted. Two teenage soldiers from the other side of the world, accustomed now to daily death and destruction, letting their hair down for a while. Jack described it as 'hectic delight', without going into details.

A show, a lobster supper, a last night of beds and sheets in a London hotel and they were back on French soil again and into the slaughterhouse or holocaust, or killing fields, or whatever you like to call it. They shook hands and reported to their respective batteries.

Jack Duffell rejoined his battery on July 25. In his absence the brigade had been engaged for three days in one of the fiercest battles of the Flanders campaign and was about to take part in a new offensive. Two mounds of earth behind Jack's old D gun covered the remains of two of his old mates. Two others were in hospital, one minus a leg. Gunner Duffell was now the sole survivor of the original detachment of *Berrima* boys.

It is a wonder Jack could find the time or the energy to write during the next two months of incessant action—but he did, and one gets a vivid and sometimes harrowing account of it all through a combination of his letters and his Postscript.

He wrote his letters under all conditions, sometimes crouched in muddy dug-outs, his well-worn pencil grasped tightly in his fingers as German shells whistled overhead. The 'little Welch girl', Cassie Harris, begins to figure in his letters sending him letters, parcels and photographs.

In the field
    7-8-17
Dear Mother Dad Sis & Bro

Here we are again dears, still hanging on to this old world & going strong. It is not long since I last wrote but I thought you would be wondering how things were going for I expect you read the latest. Came down yesterday for a couple of days spell at waggon lines so I am in J.Ps. humpy for a night or two. He had a great time in Blighty he says & like me found it hard to settle down when he got back. I have not heard from the other three for a couple of weeks but am quite sure they are doing well. Mud with a capital M is in full swing again at present so of course everyone is in a good humour (I dont think) I think the bad weather will be here again before long.

Well now dears how is everyone over that way? Have you got my house yet? Don't forget that I will want a home if I bring back a little Welch girl. Wouldent the Ausie girls go pop if I did.

When I finish this I am hopping up to our Sergeant for leave to ride back a few miles & have a hot bath & get a clean unchatty change of underclothes. I don't want to go back up the line in this lot if I can help it.

Well I will ring off as I want to wait till the mail comes in before I write a long letter so please remember me to all & keep my best love & kisses for yourselves. Bye Bye for the present dears

XXXXXXXXXX Your Loving Son & Bro Jack

In the field
    17-8-17
Dear Old Dad

its some time since you had a letter all to yourself so here we are still in one piece & dodging them like a gooden. Well Dad I suppose you will see the news the paper had at this date so you will know things are rather willing that's why I am writing so often for I know what things you will be thinking. When I finish Ill have an hours nap for there was little sleeping time last night or for the last week in fact. Have not had a wash or shave for 6 days so you will be able to guess what your Son Johny looks like. Am living in hopes of a couple of days at the waggon line shortly for you know it knocks hell out of a fellow not getting his sleep. Never mind I'll sleep for a week when I get back to old Ausie.

Had a letter from Frank & Bob a few days back & to use their own words 'they have deemed it necessary to declare war again' & they are now back in France & I suppose by this well in it. Frank is trying to take

Bob back with him to his battery so when Fred comes back we will be in twos J.P. was OK when I last saw him & I intend wringing his neck a little next time I see him for he has not sent me any smokes up. Out of action I smoke about a packet a week but in places like these I get through 4 or five.

A few nights back I received a parcel from the little Welch girl containing a couple packets of smokes a home made sponge cake about 2 lbs weight & some chocolate. Did well dont you think? It could not have come at a more welcome moment for at the time I was hunched up in a muddy dug-out half wet & hungery and nearly smokeless so you see I fell right on my feet.

I wonder what has become of all the mail lately. It seems ages since I had a letter from home. Perhaps there will be a mail in a few days. In last letter I received those addresses of Don Brays but of course they were too late so next time I'm in Blighty I may want them.

Well now Dad how is everything doing at the little home. I suppose that Railway cove is on strike with the rest of the rotters. They ought to shove a heavy barrage over the rotters I reckon. I am off for a bit of a sleep now so please pass on a kiss each to all & my best love too. Bye Bye from Son John XXXXXXXXXX

In the field
   20-8-17
Dear Mother Dad Sis & Bro.

am at the waggon line for a couple of days to have a wash shave & sleep etc. Yesterday a mail came in & I got four letters & 2 were from you. I was so pleased to hear from you all again as it seemed a terrible long time since the last mail arrived. Glad you are all well dears & am glad to hear that Dad is able to do a bit.

Am OK myself again now that Ive had a good sleep & a bath & change of underclothes. For 7 nights I spent a fairly rough time for there was no time for sleep & when there was it was only sitting room with a mud carpet. However it will be better this time for the sun has been out this last few days.

Am getting on 'Tres Bein' with my limber gunnery job. I told you I think before that I had taken a limber gunners job. You know one man has to be responsible for keeping the contraption in order. I assure you I am getting good oh at pulling her to pieces & by getting it all back without a surplus. Its an oily job but I like it & a chap learns a little from it . . .

Well now dears its parade time so I will have to close up & go & clean my gun I do that instead of turning in to stables.

Well here we are again just had tea consisting of sardines & bread & jam so Im feeling in nick for letter writing. There was more mail in this afternoon but I missed this time. Jack is waiting to write but I have his pencil so he will have to wait till I have finished.

I see you are getting the cold weather over that side. I would rather you had it than us anyhow for it will not be half as bad as our Winter. It won't be long before we have it though for we can notice it getting cooler every day. . .

Oh Gee Whiz have just been given an hour to be ready to go up again so I'll have to close dears. With best love to all & heaps of kisses.

> I remain
> Your Loving Son & Bro
> Jack

> In the field
> 29th 8-1917

Dear Mother Dad Sis & Bro

Five minutes ago I received your ever welcome letter dated 24th June & now I'm sitting down or rather crouching down to answer it. I'm in the line dears & have been for several days. Came up from the W.L. the following day after writing last letter I think. Yes dears I'm quite well still but a bit done up but we can't expect anything else seeing that sleep has been almost out of the question for the past 4 days. All the same we manage to keep a smile up & sometimes a song.

At present there is nothing doing for an hour or so, so I am well down in a dug out that will stop a fair shell & when Ive finished writing will try & have a sitting down sleep. I suppose you will think thats a terrible state of affairs but its really nothing these times.

Jack P. has just sent me a couple of pairs of dry sox & some eatables up from the waggon line so Ill be able to change my wet sox. Only been wet three days. Just as well you are a good way off when my boots come off. I dont mind how many sox you send me dears for winter is on the way again & they will all be needed. It has been very cold these last few days raining & blowing too.

I am glad in one way that I have kept going through it all even if its only to prove that those who said I could not stand the strain are liars.

I got the little spray of wattle dears & it reminds me more & more of dear old Ausie. Perhaps it won't be long before I am back picking my own wattle & button holes. Keep the red rose going. Jessie told me about going to see you Mum & she said it was like going to her own home. I write to her you know. In fact I write to a lot of girls so I hope they don't all get serious at once. I'll stand them perhaps one at a time.

You say Mum that you hope I write every week. Well dears you can always rest assured that I will never let a week go if I can help it. I dont always get your letters but I know you write just the same. Our mail gets a rough spin I think.

I see Dad has been putting in some good work in the gardening department. I'm sorry I can't send you a few huns over Dad but by the look of them when our boys bring them in you would not get much work out of them. One cuss had the hide to want a cigarette one day & had been dodging his damn whis bangs all the morning without a smoke for myself.

Fancy the boy going messages by himself. (That's the way kid, help Mother). I can see myself sparing up with threepence every time he cleans my boots for he seems to have his head screwed on the right way for making money.

Well now dear all I will close up for the time being & next time I write I hope we will be out resting well back somewhere. Remember me to all & share my best love & kisses

Bye Bye with love to all
from Son & Bro
Jack XXXX

Jack's next letter gave just a hint of foreboding that his good luck and charmed life might not last forever. He had on many occasions emphasised to his family that he stood as much chance as anyone else of surviving. But as the boys fell around him in increasing numbers, his faith in his philosophy faltered as his chances diminished. It was unusual for him to share such thoughts with his mother, though he apologised to her for bringing up the subject.

In the field
6-9-17

Dear Mother Dad Sis & Bro

Here we are again still able to sit up & take nourishment. Well dears since last letter I have received your letter dated 17th of June & the mail before that. I received yours of the 24th so you see dears we get our mail anyhow now days. Never mind though as long as some word comes I am satisfied.

I have got a spell for a couple of days in the waggon lines. Can assure you I am feeling a lot better after a deacent sleep for a few nights. You see when all the boys went out I came in for all the work doing both laying & limber gunner as well. Hope I finished off a few hundred huns. It gets quite exciting pelting them over at Fritz & he returning the compliment. You would not believe the 'don't care a hang' sensation that comes over a chap when in action under fire. It's after it's all over that you feel it...

How did Dad get on at the Barracks about changing the allotment? I will try again to have it altered for now that winter is coming on I would like a little more cash. My book is still over drawn so I can only draw 2 bob a week.

If they will not alter the allotment Mum do you think its asking too much to send another ten pounds to the commonwealth bank London in case anything happens & I get over again.

There has been a lot of Blighty wounds flying about & I would not like to be stranded in Hospital with an overdrawn book. Of course I don't think anything of the kind will happen, but I am the last of our original detachment & one never knows. I don't like to have to write like that Mum but you will understand I know...

Kiss the nipps for me please & share my best love all round.

Bye Bye for the present

from Son & Bro

XXXX Jack XXXX

10

Not to Reason Why

The 'stunt' Gunner Duffell and his brigade were engaged in was to become known as the Third Battle of Ypres, or simply Passchendaele. The British military writer, Sir Basil Liddell Hart, described it after the war as the 'last scene of the gloomiest drama in British military history'. There is scathing criticism of Field Marshal Haig in Liddell Hart's classic *History of the First World War*, first published in 1930, twelve years after the war had ended, and reprinted many times since.

Despite misgivings by the British Cabinet, Haig had insisted on pressing ahead with his plan for a knock-out blow against the Germans in the autumn of 1917. The Cabinet wished to postpone serious operations until the French had recovered and the Americans had arrived on the scene and to save their strength until 1918. Haig, however, had an optimistic belief that he could defeat the German armies single-handed in Flanders. It was a plan founded on faith rather than reason, Liddell Hart wrote, and both plan and faith were to be sunk in the mud of Flanders:

Passchendaele has come to be, like Walcheren a century before, a synonym for military failure—a name black-bordered in the records of the British Army. Even the inexhaustible powers of endurance and sacrifice shown by the combatants or the improved executive leadership which did much in the later stages to minimise their sufferings, tend to be not merely overshadowed, but eclipsed in memory by the futility of the purpose and result.

The offensive was doomed before it began, Liddell Hart maintained, if only because of a legend that the ill-famed 'swamps of Passchendaele' were due to heavy rain. In reality, the area had been reclaimed from marshland by centuries of labour and in consequence the farmers of the district were under penalty to keep their dykes clear. If the drainage were to be destroyed by heavy bombardment the battlefield would become a swamp again. Haig was warned about this, but he ignored it.

British artillery strength along the eighteen-kilometre front totalled 3,091 guns, of which 999 were heavy. The bombardment for Haig's offensive opened on 22 July and lasted for ten days. With an average of one gun to every six metres of the front, four and a quarter million shells were fired during the bombardment, representing four and three-quarter tonnes thrown for every metre of the front. Then at 3.50 a.m. on 31 July the infantry of twelve divisions, including Australians, advanced to the accompaniment of torrential rain.

The Germans retaliated with mustard gas and new methods of defence and attack. Little ground was won but casualties were horrific.

Liddell Hart says that Haig continued to send the War Office confident reports that the enemy were 'fast approaching' the exhaustion of their forces. Actually, the Germans were making preparations not only to attack the Russians in Riga, but to crush the Italians by sending eight or ten divisions to reinforce the Austrians.

Haig refused to be dissuaded from his purpose. A second blow against the Germans on 16 August was a diminished replica of the first in its results. The army was bogged down again, with high casualties. Other attacks on 26 September and 24 October near Ypres had better success, despite torrents of rain. Some prestige was restored, but it had little effect on a campaign that was foredoomed and, according to Liddell Hart:

When on November 4, a sudden advance...gained the empty satisfaction of occupying the site of Passchendaele village, the official curtain was at last rung down on the pitiful tragedy of 'Third Ypres'. It was a long-overdue close of a campaign which had brought the British armies to the verge of exhaustion, one in which had been enacted the most dolorous scenes in British military history. The only justification evoked the reply that, in order to absorb the enemy's attention and forces, Haig chose the spot most difficult for himself and least vital to his enemy.

Perhaps the most damning comment on the plan which plunged the British Army in this bath of mud and blood is contained in an incidental revelation of the remorse of one who was largely responsible for it.

This highly placed officer from General Headquarters was on his first visit to the battle front—at the end of the four months' battle. Growing increasingly uneasy as the car approached the swamplike edges of the battle area, he eventually burst into tears, crying, 'Good God, did we really send men to fight in that?' To which his companion replied that the ground was far worse ahead.

You will find none of these perspectives in Gunner Duffell's letters home. He knew nothing of the high strategy of the battle; he left those things to 'The Heads', as he called them. His job was not to reason why but to keep pumping shells in amongst the Germans until he fell back exhausted and was relieved. His was the odd one gun out of the 3,091 guns laying down the barrage. Besides, he did not want to worry his mother with the gory details.

He has left behind, however, his diaries and Postscript with all their stark reportage. Here follow some extracts from his recollections:

The Tommies (English troops) were going over at 3.30 a.m. on this morning of July 31 & after firing for an hour the teams were coming up & we were to limber up & follow up the advance. So easy to plan these things, but it so happened this was to prove our hottest & most costly stunt yet encountered.

The whistle blew & bedlam broke loose immediately. For an hour we fired & the range crept up in 50 yard hops. The teams trotted up & cease fire was ordered. In a few minutes the smoking guns were limbered up and going forward into the smoke to follow up the advancing Tommies.

The Major had gone forward some hours before to pick out a suitable new battle position but no position was picked because the Major was sniped through the head soon after he reached the front line. Also the attack by the Tommies was breaking down & not knowing anything had gone wrong the guns continued going forward. As we topped a rise close to our old front line we could see the attack breaking up & many of the Tommies coming back.

Fritz observed the advancing guns & recognising a wonderful target he at once turned his guns on us. Our colums was soon a shambles. Teams were blown to pieces & men dropped or limped away. Still the sound teams went forward & behind D gun we six gunners trudged wondering just how much further we'd get before one of those limb tearing shells would send us to eternity.

Jack's worst fears were confirmed when, less than four hours later, D gun was blown to pieces along with five of the crew. Gunner Duffell was now the sole crew survivor.

Someone called my name & I found it was Jack Harris my leave mate who being sent over to our Battery on a message was looking me up. He informed me he was the last but one of his signallers. Neither of us expected to see the day out, but he grinned a so long at me & was gone into the smoke.

By dark half the crews were wiped out & 2 more guns had gone. There were now 3 guns left. I joined one of the crews & somehow stayed alive. After dark those of us who had seen the day out were ordered back to Railway dug outs about a mile back. The guns behind had taken over our sector. That is they fired from the rear position onto the country we had been covering during the day. We were to have a nights rest. We needed it.

That rest was short-lived. At about 11 p.m. Jack was shaken awake, summoned to the battery commander and ordered to take despatches to artillery offices in a dugout close behind the front line. He and another gunner, Ted, were given a torch each and told to go on their way:

'Report to me when you get back,' the commander said.

'IF we get back,' Ted commented drily.

We were shown a map & from that were supposed to find the place three miles away on a pitch black night. As we trudged through the night we cursed the war & those responsible for it.

Passing the battery position we had vacated earlier in the evening we were met by the man on guard there who informed us that Fritz had been shelling ever since we left & that 2 more guns were blown out.

Wishing him luck and with a joking remark to keep his head down we made forward. Following the directions of a trench map in daylight is difficult enough but trying the same thing on a dark night is almost impossible. Soon we were lost & only the flares from the front line kept us going in the right direction. Soon Ted fell & lost his torch in the mud.

A trench that appeared to be leading forward we followed but soon the reek of freshly shelled earth & the torn condition of the land close by told the story. Fritz had been onto that trench & it had been dealt with properly. From one hole to another we stumbled.

I tripped over something & the torch went spinning away into the mud. In getting up I felt the object I had fallen over, it was a body and not yet stiff. The metal buttons on the tunic told me it was a Tommy who had died there. He was not the only one either as further on we found more & more. The poor devils had been caught in that shallow trench & had suffered heavily. 'Let us get out of this' I said to Ted, 'These poor cows are getting on my nerves'.

Making over the top & toward the trench flares we tried to get bearings. A figure loomed up in the darkness. It was a Tommy, he did his best to direct us to the position we sought so we thanked him & plodded on & finally found the officers & handed over the despatch. A sergeant noting we were about all in & came to light with a fair tot of rum & some ideal milk. It was a gift from heaven.

It was close to daylight by the time Ted & I reported back to the Captain. Ted had the bright idea that there might be a bottle of whisky in the Captain's mess dug out. We found ½ a bottle of Black & White & had a good swig each. There wasn't much left so we decided to finish it off. My last recollection of that night was rolling up in that wet blanket & to all sense & purpose just died.

As the weeks sent by, the brigade continued to suffer grevious losses of men and guns. Jack received another welcome visit from Jack Harris, 'still going strong', and they exchanged greetings and cigarettes.

One particular night was to stay in Jack's memory 'like a terrible dream'. He was on the midnight shift of what was known as 'S.O.S. and gas guard':

The crews were sleeping in dugouts dug in the side of a shallow trench. Fritz had started early in the evening to shell the positions with 'Whis bang' (shrapnel). The air seemed full of whistling metal & as I walked up & down behind those dugouts with the sleeping men who were depending on me to wake them if gas shells came over I could feel my nerve going. My worst fear was that I would break down & run.

After about an hour of it one of the boys who had had a good sleep, came out & offered to take my place for an hour while I had a sleep. I think that man saved me making a fool of myself or worse perhaps.

There were 4 more killed & 4 wounded during the next day but the guns escaped. On the night of the 16th we fired on a stunt for the Tommy infantry. They advanced 2 thousand yards but were pushed back to the original line by the morning. The Tommies did not seem to have the knack of holding won ground like the Aussie infantry.

After a short action on the night of the 17th, I had remained at the gun pit after the crew had crawled away to a dugout. Cleaned the breech mechanism etc & hastened away to cover myself. We had built our sleeping dugouts some hundred yards to the flank of the position, a trench running from the dugouts & behind the guns.

As I hurried along the top a close approaching shell caused me to jump into the trench. I landed on someone at the bottom of the trench. There was no curse but the shell burst close by. As the clods & earth ceased falling I flashed my torch on the silent figure & met the glassy stare of a young fellow who had left Australia in the same reinforcements as me.

I had not seen him since landing in Egypt till that night. Next day I buried him & placed some empty shell cases to mark the spot. Over a year later when I returned to Sydney a list of missing men was handed me & there appeared the name of the man I had buried by Sanctuary Wood. His parents then knew the fate of their missing son.

A stunt started at 7 AM & we were just in time to get the gun going & had the satisfaction of seeing the Tommies take Inverness Copse & a good haul of prisoners. I remember those prisoners & the regretable incident that happened.

As they were escorted back past the guns one group strung out in single file passed in front of the guns instead of behind. I was laying & firing at the time. The sergeant yelled & shouted to the guard to make the huns lie down & crawl past. The Tommy in charge did not hear or understand & the rate of fire had to be kept up.

After vain attempts by the sergeant to get the prisoners down he ordered me to fire. Closing my eyes I pulled the firing lever. They were down & scrambling & crawling past when I again looked.

Later in the day one of my crew stopped a nasty lump of five nine with his arm & to my joy & relief I was ordered to take him back to the dressing station & then report to the waggon line.

Only for one day though as 4 more guns arrived & we took them back into action at once & fired most of the day. I fired 300 rounds for my days work & went on S O S & gas guard at night. Still the shelling kept us on the hop & although the pits & ammunition were damaged the guns remained intact. Rain fell most of the time & a strong wind blew up.

There was some blessed relief for Gunner Duffell in September when he was sent to a workshop behind the lines with some damaged guns. During five days of bliss while the guns were being repaired, he made the acquaintance of a 'very pretty Belgium shopgirl in the town who spoke excellent English'.

'Even evening I spent hours by a warm fireside & ate good and well-cooked meals,' he wrote. 'The father and his 2 daughters who were refugees from the early days of the hun invasion kept this shop. I have happy recollections of the evenings spent in their company.'

Then it was back to the front and the carnage again:

The ruined town of Ypres loomed out of the darkness & soon we were passing the remains of the Cathedral & the Cloth Hall. Heavy shells roared into the ruins at intervals. As we passed out of the town on the Menin Road a traffic officer stopped the column & informed the Major that the storage & ammunition dumps at 'Hellfire' corner were on fire & advised him not to try & take the teams through. 'These guns must be in action before morning' replied the Major.

Down the cobble road about ½ mile ahead we could see the dumps blazing on each side of the road. Teams were ordered to keep 100 yards behind each other & go through at the gallop. First went A Sub & when they had the 100 yards start the next team set off.

It came D subs turn & I glanced at the face of the gunner riding on the gun limber beside me. He was one of the new reinforcements & had not seen action as yet. His face was white & set. I could not see mine.

As we came abreast of the burning dump the heat was stifling & up above a hun plane was flying & dropping bombs. C Subs ammunition team ahead of our team suddenly went down in a heap a bomb had found them.

We galloped over the struggling horses & men & the reinforcements exclaimed 'My God does it get any worse than this?' 'This is nothing' I answered. Had to say something but I was just as scared as that new hand. With the exception of that one team the battery got through & hell fire corner (well named) was behind us.

Next morning 4th Oct we opened up at 5.30 to cover our own Aussie Infantry in their first attack of the series that took place in that section. Soon the range crept up & we knew they were going ahead & more country was being taken from Fritz. Just to the left of the position a duck board track wound round the shell holes & supporting Infantry used this track as they trudged in single file to the forward area.

During the morning batches of hun prisoners were brought back, many of them being wounded. Wounded Aussies also made their way back & it was no uncommon sight to see our wounded being assisted by a couple of Fritzies. All day both wounded Aussies & prisoners in ever increasing numbers passed the gun position & were often caught in the shell fire that the battery positions were being subjected to. Two more of our gunners were wounded during the day but no guns in the 2nd battery were hit. Rain fell incessantly.

During the night we fired on the counter attacking enemy but they did not dislodge our men & towards daylight the firing eased down & we gunners had a couple of hours sleep in the mud. It was impossible to build dry sleeping possies & the weather was becoming cold. I dreaded the thoughts of another winter in action.

11

A Charmed Life

Jack did his best to maintain his weekly quota of letters to Hurstville during Haig's four-month battle of attrition, but it wasn't easy. Still, there were occasional rest periods when he was able to pull out the pencil and write home. On 15 September and in an understatement of the year, he excused himself by saying, 'I never seem to have any news'. No news!

John Polson has stuck to me all the time (you know this business has made Jack quite a different man to what I expected him to be).

You should see the pair of us smoking our pipes & arguing the point. Now and then we have what is termed a rough house & start wrestling and knocking things about. We generally finish up by getting pitched out by the other chaps in the tent.

Oh yes we are quite happy or I should say as circs. permit & am making the best of things. We are out resting about 3 miles away from a fairly big town & so far we have had two afternoons in together. Yesterday we had a fish & chips tea & it was Tres Bein but not the sort that Mother makes all the same. . .

I thought of a lot of things to write about when I was doing my shift between 12 & 3 a.m. but now its all gone out of my head. I think I am slipping back a lot in the letter writing line. One time I could sit down & write till further orders but now I never seem to have any news.

The mails seemed to provide the morale backbone for his resolution and determination to stay alive. He kept a detailed diary of postings and receipts of letters and parcels to and from 'dear old Ausie'. In one letter he was enraged by the actions of 'parcel pinchers' at army administrative headquarters behind the lines:

Somewhere in France 21-9-17

Dear Mother Dad Sis & Bro.

another week has gone & I am still as well as they make em. Hope you can all say the same in the little Grey home. Well dears just after I posted the last letter a mail came in & I received your letter dated 31-6-17 & I mentioned receiving the 8-7-17 a few days before so you see the mail has been slightly mixed as per usual.

I also received one parcel which I mentioned but you sent two so one is still coming (or most likely gone) I would like to catch some of the parcel pinchers. The rotters never go near the line & they can always get things that we can't & yet they take the only good things that a fellow gets in the line. Never mind every dog has his day. Well dears I am back resting still & am feeling fit for another go like the last if need be so you need not worry about my health department...

I was sorry to hear of young Payne going down. I could see by your letter Mum when you say that you would be wondering who was next that you were thinking things. Well forget those things Mother for Son Johnie has been at the game too long now to be caught napping & I'm just the kid that can duck into a shell hole with the best of them when he sends anything over. As long as he misses with the first I'm set for I'm not there for the next 'oh no' not John.

I'm sorry that you took what I said about Dad's illness to heart Mum but I did not mean that you were telling lies you know. I only thought that you were making light of it so that I would not worry. I'm sorry Mum that I mentioned it at all, but call it square & it won't happen again.

Thank all the kind friends for me Mum who are knitting sox. They are the main items in Winter & by the looks of things we are in for another one very soon. The nights & mornings are pretty crisp even now.

There seems to be a terrible fuss made over this Les Darcy too. When a man comes over here & stops one he stops here permanent but if a man runs away & kicks the bucket they take him home & make a fuss of him. Someone has slipped back.

(Les Darcy was a twenty-two year-old middleweight boxing champion who skipped Australia in October 1916. He died in America in May 1917, from blood poisoning. In *This Fabulous Century*, Peter Luck says there was little doubt that strings were pulled to prevent him fighting in America; the Australian government could not afford to let him become a hero. Though condemned by many as a war 'shirker', the Irish community made a martyr of Darcy. More than 100,000 people viewed his embalmed body when it was brought back to Australia in June 1917.)

Well now how is the little grey home getting on? Tell the young lady that she may have my room. John is pitching tent on the side lawn later on. By gee I would like to see the boy, he must be a regular young devil. I can see he is a dinkim young 'jam buck'. Lill is still sticking to you. I suppose she is quite a big girl by this.

Fancy your Son nearly 20 you will have to have an extry keg ready for me when I get back. Well I will close up now dear all so please share my best love & kisses.

Bye Bye for the week
from Son & Bro
Jack XXXXXXXXX

On 9 October, the eve of his twentieth birthday, Jack wrote home with the news that he would be spending it on his gun in the front line. It would be different to his nineteenth, when he was kicked in the ribs by a horse, but not to worry.

He also pondered on what official manhood on the following year would mean to him, having left the teens behind, before expressing some angry comments on the widespread industrial strife in Australia. It had begun in August with railwaymen downing tools because they objected to a fresh system of time-cards. They asserted that this would lead to speeding-up and other undesirable things. The strike was eventually broken, largely by volunteer strike breakers from all sections of Australian society. In the cold and mud of France, Jack referred to the strikers as 'skunks'. He was not to know that one of them was a locomotive driver named Ben Chifley, a future prime minister of Australia. (Chifley was dismissed but later reinstated, on appeal, but only as a fireman.)

In the field
9-10-17

Dear Mother Dad Sis & Bros.

Here we are again still going strong & as well as ever in spite of the rain & wind. Well dears I am out of it for a couple of days for a spell at the waggon lines. I put in 9 days at the guns with wet feet & clothes

An Australian transport wagon on the road near Red Lodge, behind Hill 63, in Belgium, while the Germans were shelling batteries of the Australian and New Zealand artillery concentrated there for the Battle of Messines in 1917 (AWM negative no. E650)

The ruins of the famous Cloth Hall at Ypres in Belgium, photographed on November 5, 1917. Gunner Duffell was engaged in fierce artillery duels in this area (AWM negative E1230)

Mary Dircks

Farmer Duffell carried his bride over the entrance to this tent on his Yenda farm after their marriage in 1921

Lieutenant (later Captain) Duffell served in the Volunteer Defence Force in World War II

& little cover from the rain & cold but a couple of nights back was relieved for a couple of days so of course I am living with Jack & Bert Dorman & am feeling as well & fit as ever again.

I intended writing to you tomorrow same as I did last Brithday but I am afraid I will be going up again tonight or early in the morning so this Birthday will be nothing like the last. Never mind with a little luck we may spend the next together.

I do want to be home when I become a man. I don't know how a man should feel but I think I am just the same Johnie that I was 2 years ago except that I believe I have a little more sense & have learnt to 'look before I leap'. I have lost that hot headedness, for it does not pay in this business.

Well now dears I wrote once while at the position but now I am answering the heap of letters that came a couple of days back. Those letters that I thought had gone astray turned up at last. 'These dates' 17.7.16 22.7.17 29.7.17 5.8.17 & 11.8.17, there are still a few missing.

What a rotten lot those Railway mob are. The skunks grumble for nothing. Just as well the boys over this side don't look at hardships etc in the same light as that mob. Even if they do have a crook spin at times they always have a home to go to with a good bed & plenty to eat. We have things a bit rougher than they & no home except a couple of water proofs & a few sand bags. That has to stop shells etc as well as rain. Perhaps the strikers would like to change places for a while. . .

Mary Dircks sent her photo along last mail & its very nice, I reckon. Did you get my letter saying that I had altered my allotment? so I will be drawing two shillings per day after the 30th November. Well now dear all I have told you all the news so I will have to conclude with Tons of love & kisses to all

from Son & Bro

XXXXXX

Jack XXXXXX

Gunner Duffell was lucky indeed to survive until his twentieth birthday. A German shell exploded beside the dugout in which he and another gunner were sheltering at night and they were buried alive in debris for ten minutes, the longest minutes of their lives. They were dug out just in time.

Earlier in the day he had received another shock. 'I walked over to the 3rd Battery to see Jack Harris,' he was to write. 'One of the sergeants told me that Jack had been blown to pieces a few days before. One gets used to seeing his mates going West, but it was with a heavy heart that

I made my way back to my possie, wondering how I would break the news to his relations in Wales.'

He wrote a brief letter home about his birthday five days later. For some reason, he waited another week before mentioning that he and two others had been recommended for the Military Medal, the medal for bravery for soldiers below commissioned rank. But only one was to be awarded and he missed out. On the same day, he was promoted to Bombardier, which carried a stripe and a pay increase. The rank, however, was subject to confirmation, which would take a week or two.

In the field

15.10.17

Dear Mother Dad Sis & Bro.

just a short note this time dears to let you know that I got through last stunt alright. Hope dears that you are all quite OK. Well dears when I last wrote you remember it was the day before my birthday & I was expecting to go up to the guns.

Well I did go up & this is how I spent my Birthday. Started out in the morning & trudged through some 5 miles of mud to the position. On arriving found Fritz making a butcher's shop of the place with high explosive. That ment dodging about in the rain most of the day.

Towards night when things got quieter I turned in to the blankets in a small dug out with one of the boys & some time through the night (Blank) put one alongside & brought the show in on top of us you see dears it was an exciting pleasant birthday.

Never mind though I got out of it alright & am now back at the WL enjoying another couple of days rest. Some more of the boys went out to it but John kept the old flag flying.

Am living with J.P of course while I am down here & last night he received a parcel from home & you should have seen us getting in on some plum pudding with condensed milk over it. Your Birthday parcels have not arrived yet Mum but I expect them anytime now & you can rest assured that I will do justice to the contents.

I had a letter from one of my old gun mates yesterday he is being sent back to Ausie through wounds received out of the Stunt I hit when I came back from Blighty. He tells me that Fred will be back here again before long. Hope he gets back to the same gun as me for I am the only one left out of the crew we had when he went away. He was the first to go.

Well now dears I am going to close up but will write again as soon

as I get some mail so Bye Bye for the time being & please remember
me to all the relations & friends

With best Love & Kisses to all

I Remain

Am wishing you a   Your Loving Son & Bro

Merry Xmas & a   XXXXX   Jack

Happy New Year in   XXXXX

all letters in case

you do not get one

of them

Jack never wrote to his parents about the events of the day after his
birthday, but he told about it in his Postscript. It seemed that he was
leading a charmed life.

By daylight all hands were moving about the pits & it was bitterly cold.
Someone lit a fire on the semi dry ground close by the wrecked dugouts
& a dixie of water was put on to boil. A dozen or so of us crouched
on our haunches round the fire anticipating a warm drink of black tea
when the water boiled.

By a trick of fate I was called away from the fire by another limber
gunner who had suggested we two cleaned our guns up while the water
boiled. We were not 20 yards away when a big one roared at us & we
took the prone position in the mud.

As the rain of mud descended I looked towards the fire, it was gone
& the men were strewn about in the mud. Eight were alive but all badly
wounded. Bill, my dug out mate of the night before had a fearful hole
in his back.

It took some time to get them all to the dressing station & when that
was over the survivors took stock of ourselves. My team had gone &
A Sub also only had one man left & that was the limber gunner who
had coaxed me away from the fire. By a strange coincidence it was the
third time for each of us to survive the rest of the crew.

The battle for Passchendaele was nearing its bloody climax and the
Germans were about to launch new and more deadly gas attacks. And
Gunner Duffell's luck was at last about to run out.

12

A Devilish Incense

Both sides used poison gas in World War I. The Germans tried many experiments and their first battlefield attack with it was a failure. They fired 3,000 shrapnel shells containing a nose and eye irritant as well as bullets, but with little success. In January 1915 they tried an improved lachrymatory gas shell in an attack against the Russians in Poland. This also failed because of the nullifying effect of the intense cold on the gas.

The next German attempt was at Ypres in April 1915, and this time it was nearly a war-winner. Lethal chlorine gas was discharged from cylinders with devastating success. A strange greenish-white fog drifted into the Allied lines and threw the agonised defenders into chaos. British, French and African troops, none of whom had respirators, fled back in terror and distress, leaving a gap in the front line more than six kilometres wide. The Germans missed their chance by failing to have adequate reserves to exploit the unforeseen breakthrough.

Haig hit back in April 1917, when a new British gas shell was most effective in paralysing the enemy artillery. It not only compelled gun crews to keep their gas masks on for hours at a time but killed off the horses like flies and prevented ammunition being brought up. In June and July the Germans responded with the introduction of mustard gas, a new terror which interfered seriously with British artillery and concentration areas. However, gas remained a difficult weapon to control. During the Battle of Loos, in September 1917, the British discharged nearly 150 tonnes of gas from 5,000 cylinders. Anxiety and misjudgment about the wind directions bedevilled the operation. Much of the deadly cloud drifted back towards the Allied lines and many of the infantry were poisoned by their own gas.

Liddell Hart described chlorine gas as having the 'smell of devilish incense'. On the moralistic side he had this to say:

The chlorine gas originally used was undeniably cruel, but not worse than the frequent effect of shell or bayonet, and when it was succeeded by improved forms of gas both experience and statistics proved it the least inhumane of modern weapons. But it was novel and therefore labelled as an atrocity by a world which condones abuses but detests innovation. Thus Germany incurred the moral odium which inevitably accompanies the use of a novel weapon without any compensating advantage.

One could perhaps equate this argument with the use of atomic weapons today.

It was unfortunate for Gunner Duffell that his artillery brigade was engaged in a battle that saw the Germans introduce a new and improved (from the killing point of view) method of gas attack.

The Germans masked their new assault with heavy bombardments of high explosives, then throwing in 'sneezing gas' which rendered it difficult for soldiers to keep on their respirators. They then changed to mustard gas, forcing their enemy to wear gas masks throughout the whole bombardment, precluding sleep. Severe bombardments of back areas with mustard gas continued almost nightly throughout October and early November. The valleys behind the lines were drenched with mustard gas.

Dr C.E.B. Bean, in his *Official History of Australia in the War of 1914–18*, described the attacks as a 'dreadful success'. The Australian field artillery brigades had already suffered heavy casualties from gas. They had lost 148 casualties in July, 38 in August, 100 in September, 501 in October and were to lose 526 in November. The condition of the worst cases was 'pitiful', Bean reported. Two batteries of 'Jack's mob', 1st Australian Field Artillery Brigade, were put out of action on Anzac Ridge on the night of 28 October. Five days later the commanders of two more batteries were gassed and died within forty-eight hours.

That same night, 2 November, was the night Gunner Duffell's luck ran out, too. Jack tells about the lead-up to it in his Postscript. By this time, he had been constantly in action for eighteen months, except for a few breaks of a week or so while the battery rested or reorganised after each battle. Casualties had reduced the normal ten-man strength of his gun crew to a sergeant, two gunners and himself:

It was bad enough to be under constant shell fire, but working so short handed was taking toll of both nerves and strength. Each night we were kept very much on the alert owing to gas. Most nights at some period gas masks would have to be worn, sometimes for hours. This of course meant very little sleep. . .

All day on October 21 the woods and the surrounding country were heavily shelled. Guns were going to pieces but old D gun came through with only a shaking. We were warned that we were to be duty gun for the night & would be required to fire two short shoots of 20 rounds at 2 hours intervals.

The sergeant and I decided to split the duty, I was to take one gunner & fire the first 20 rounds & two hours later he would take the other gunner & fire the last shoot. We were to fire on a crossroad a couple of miles back behind the German line. The target had been registered during the day so we knew the range etc.

At eight p.m. I took my pre-war mate Fred who had lately rejoined us after a spell in hospital & the pair of us waded through the mud to the gun & setting the 20 shells to the correct fuze loaded up. Fred took over the range wheel & breech lever while I laid & fired the gun. We were to get the 20 rounds off as quickly as possible, the idea being to catch troops & transport teams under our spray of shrapnel.

It was no easy task for only 2 of us as the gun was worn & did not run back far enough after the recoil & it took our combined strength to push the breach back after every shot. After a few rounds our eyes began to smart & water & we knew the gun had mustard gas sprayed over it, probably from some of the shells that had come over earlier in the night. Putting on our gas masks we completed the shoot & cleaned the gun out.

Fred & the other gunner a new hand were to take turns at SOS gas guard for the night. Fred took the first watch for 2 hours & the rest of us turned in to sleep. At 10.30 the sergeant was awakened & off he went with the new hand to fire his 20 rounds onto those poor devils of huns back on the crossroad.

When they returned I posted the new man on his job as guard & warning him to awaken me at the first smell of gas which would have the smell of ripe pineapples, left him outside & lay down again. My stripe excused me from any more duties such as guard or fatigues, but of course had to take charge of guards etc. This night though I was not to have rest. The new man being unaquainted with the smell of gas woke me three or four times during the first hours. He imagined every taint in the air to be poison gas.

At last I decided to stay out myself & sent him into the pill box. Had he remained on duty for another ten minutes or so he would have been in no doubt about the presence of gas.

A shower of popping gas shells had landed in the wood quite close to us & at once the yellow green haze began to spred death to those unwary ones caught asleep or without gas masks. A yell woke the three in the pill box & dragging on my mask, made for another pill box some distance away where I knew some officers to be.

I didn't reach them as the darkness & mud & barbed wire frustrated my efforts. As my feet tangled in the wire beneath a foot of mud I was helpless & better to see I pulled my gas mask off for a moment. That moment was almost fatal as the gas was drifting in a dense cloud & it caught my breath before I could pull the mask on again. It was a deadly feeling & as I was dragged into the pill box iron bands appeared to tighten round my chest & I felt as though I must choke. Ammonia phials were broken under my nose & gradually I got my breath back but my voice had gone & I was almost blind.

Next morning I was led back out of the forward area, first to the waggon line where I was placed on horse back & led off to a dressing station & picked up by an ambulance & by night placed on a stretcher in the field hospital at Poperinghe.

During the night together with other wounded I was carried to a hospital train which steamed toward the coast. As I lay in that bunk the sounds of war gradually faded from hearing & I fell asleep till daylight. Where I was I knew not, neither did I care. I was a very sick man.

After some delay A.M.C. orderlies began to carry the wounded from the train & soon I was being put to bed in ward 59 at Etaples Base Hospital. My chest throat & eyes were burning & every intake of breath seemed to seer through my lungs. With shaded eyes I lay there while being washed & cleansed of the dirt & mud that I had collected in the slush hole up the line.

Something in a feeding bottle was brought to me but I could not swallow & waved the nurse away. At the moment I would have gone West without any qualms at all. Mentaly I cursed the gunners who fired those gas shells over & I was pleased to reflect that out of the thousands of shells I had sent over to Fritz not one had been a gas shell. Of all the horrors of war gas is the hell of it all . . .

In due course a doctor attended me & ordered drops for my eyes (Liquid fire I termed it) because it burned like sin for some time after application. The nursing sisters were wonderful and did their utmost to ease the pain of the men under their charge. They were all English girls & I hold the greatest admiration for them.

The first night brought an air raid & during the indiscriminate bomb dropping several bombs fell about the hospital & one ward was hit, with disastrous results to the inmates. The wards by the way were flimsy huts composed of wood & canvas & were far from bomb proof. It seemed that war was still on my trail.

Next day when the doctor visited me again & after a brief examination he informed the matron that I was to be sent to hospital in England. About midnight I was again lifted onto a stretcher & carried to another hospital train & was soon travelling toward the coast. Calais was reached early next morning & as we steamed onto the docks I could dimly see the hospital ship which was to carry us across the channel to England.

Well fed German prisoners were employed in carrying the wounded from the train to the ship & I smiled with satisfaction as two burly huns carried my stretcher & gently lifted me into a bunk on the ship.

As my eyes were still shaded I could not see much & anyhow I cared little at not being able to see the last of France as the ship steamed away. The rolling of the ship on top of my gas caused a bout of sea sickness which seemed to be tearing my heart out. The short crossing to Dover proved a nightmare & it was a very sick & sorry Digger who sighed with relief when the ship pulled into the wharf at Dover in England.

The wounded & sick were carried ashore on stretchers & laid in rows in a great iron shed. English women moved about the stretchers offering cigarettes etc to those inclined to smoke. Although I was longing for a smoke it was more than my throat would stand & as my eyes were still shaded I contented myself listening to the voices of those English women & thanking my stars that I was away from the mud & shells.

Eventually I was loaded into a train & late at night arrived at Clacton-on-Sea. Then followed a short run in an ambulance to Middlesex War Hospital. Before daylight next morning nurses were on the job washing the patients. My chest pained continuously & my eyes refused to open & were smarting like sin. A neat little nurse bathed them & after a treatment of drops the shade was replaced. They fed me on milk & slops which burned as I swallowed. There were eight beds in my ward, five being occupied by Australians, two by Canadians & one a tommy.

The hospital I learned had been a Womans Lunatic Asylum before the war & my seven room mates joked about the barred windows & debated the chances of sneaking out at night when they were better & able to leave the beds.

Of the eight I appeared to be worst case & was forbidden to leave my bed for anything. The visiting Doctor spoke of effected heart which did not sound good to me. The doctor ordered me away to another hospital for special heart treatment so next morning I was carried out to an ambulance & from that carried on a stretcher to a train & placed in the guards van bound for London.

In London I was carried along to the guards van of another train and taken to the No 1AA Hospital at Harefield Park in Essex. This was one of the Australian war hospitals, the Doctors & Sisters being Aussies as well as all the patients.

Special treatment consisting of steam pipes (so I called them) being pushed down by throat & plenty of eye drops etc soon had effect & in a few days I was feeling very much better & allowed to sit by a fire in the ward. The heart had not responded much to treatment so I was not permitted to move about much.

As hundreds of wounded were arriving in England after the fierce fighting at Paschendale the hospital was cleared of all except the worst cases & on the 24th November I was marked out to convalescent wards at Hurdcott near Salisbury in Wiltshire. This time I was able to walk out to the ambulance and on arrival at Hurdcott was handed over to the tender mercies of a huge Australian Sergeant Major.

The scene here was row after row of wooden huts & to one of these I was alloted, together with some 50 other rather war worn diggers. Iron bedsteads with fibre filled mattresses lined the walls & a trestle table together with forms held the centre of the hut.

A tea consisting of bread & jam followed by a rice pudding was readily despatched by the troops. Mugs & plates were washed up by the mess orderlies after which blankets were handed out three to a man. Soon all were curled up in bed as it had been a heavy day for most of us who were not yet very strong.

Hurdcott was to be Jack Duffell's 'home' for the next eight months.

13

From Mud to Mistletoe

Jack had first broken the news of his gassing to the Hurstville folk from the Poperinghe field hospital four days after it took place. Even being propped up in bed and shaded eyes could not prevent him writing letters. It was, as usual, underplayed and differed in detail from his recollections twenty-five years later:

In Dock
France 6-11-17

Dear Mother Dad Sis & Bros.

You will no doubt receive a shock to know that I am in hospital, but Fritz got home on me at last & made a blinking gas meter out of my 'bingy'. Of course things got mixed up inside & the Doc bundled me off to a dressing station from there I went to casualty clearing & after an all night trip in a hospital train I find myself in a base hospital.

I don't know if I will get any further, but am living in hopes of getting a trip to 'Blighty' out of it. Fred is in the same state as myself we both got it together. We started out together but were separated when put to bed before going on the train & I have not seen him since. No doubt he is at this hospital too but not in this Ward.

Well dears I suppose you think its awful to be gassed but both Fred & myself are only slightly effected so there is no need for you to worry. It means quite a nice spell for us out of the mud rain & cold so you see Fritz has almost done us a good turn. I reckon he is not even on me yet though for I have fired hundreds of rounds on him & know for a fact that a lot took effect...

Have not had any word of Frank or Bob for about six weeks but their crowd have been getting a rough time same as we. Well now dear all I will ring off for the present but will write again in a few days or if I get shifted.

Will wish you all a Merry Xmas & if possible a bright & peaceful New Year.

Please excuse   Best love & kisses from Son & Bro
scribble. am   Jack XXXXXXXXX
in bed with
shaded eyes.

Writing from the Middlesex War Hospital, Clacton-on-Sea, a week later, he reassured Dear Mother Dad Sis & Bro. As for the actual event that had hospitalised him, he dismissed it in a few paragraphs:

For about six nights Fritz made the place a hell with his gas. We had to have our respirators on every night and the boys were going out gallore.

About the 2nd of Nov. he finished me. I was on guard at the time & went out of the dugout to wake the Captain when the gas started & having a rotten cold at the time I started coughing & the helmet almost smothered me so I pulled it off & dived back to the dug out, but it had me wet then & when we went out for a shoot a while after & that finished the job & also most of the others too for we had to pull out of the position.

Jack was still full of high spirits in a letter from his next port of call, the Australian auxiliary hospital at Harefield Park:

No 1 AA Hospital
Harefield Park
16-11-17

Dear Mother Dad Sis & Bro

Here we are again still able to sit up and take nourishment. You see I have had a shift since writing last & am now in an Australian hospital. Everyone are Ausies. Sisters, Doctors, patients all belong to the only country in the World. By Gee its grand to see an Australian girl again and arent they different to the English girls.

Well dears I don't want you to take fright at what I tell you but it seems that the gas has effected my heart a little & I have to be very careful for a while. I feel pretty right but they won't let me get up for a while. Its not serious you know but there are a lot here like me & it only wants a spell to fix things up. I might miss the Winter through it so I think I'm lucky. . .

Have received 2 letters from Wales & they are delighted to know that I am back in England. I have 'orders' to present myself at Skewen directly my furlough starts. Of course I intend to accept their invitation for I know they will make a chap welcome.

The only bad part about this ward is that its the ward the returning men are in & there are about 14 here now & they are talking all day & all night of what they intend doing on arrival in Ausie.

Sometimes I think I'd change places with the worst case to get a look at the old place again but never mind I have high hopes of seeing the end of the war next spring. I reckon anyone who comes through the next spring offensive will see Ausie & stay there for good. I'll bet no dinkum Ausie will ever leave home again, for everyone I've met says that all the countries they have seen put together would not compare with our Ausie. They have not got a six horse team in the army that will get me to live in any of the countries I've seen while on this little joke. . .

Well now dear all I will have to close up, so please pass on my best wishes to all friends & relatives. Kiss the nipps & give them my best love. Bye Bye for the present. With best love & kisses

> I remain
> Your Loving Son & Bro
> XXXXJackXXXX

> Aust. Aux. Hospital
> Harefield
> 22.11.1917

Dear Mother Dad Sis & Bro.

here we are again almost well again. Am up & about & eating all before me. The old quack who made me out to be nearly dead wants a kick in the neck. The expected heart trouble was only slight & it does not trouble me much at all now. I am booked to kill a lot of huns yet.

Am writing pretty soon after the last letter because I wanted to ease your mind. I did not like to tell you in last letter that I expected heart trouble for I know it would worry you. The quack made it out that bad that I thought something might happen so that is why I mentioned it. They caught it in time. 'Oh gee' I had steam pipes & goodness knows what down my neck. That is all finished now & if I keep on like I'm going now, I can see myself being pitched out on furlough in less than a week. . .

I wonder if you got a cable saying that I was in hospital gassed & that I wanted £20 sent to the same place as the last. I will need some winter clothes before going back to the mud that is why I asked for £20. Hope you don't mind dears, but you would not believe how rotten it is to be here in England with no money. . .

The Battery is at present out resting & being reinforced I hear. Heard last night about our new victory on the Western front, another kick in the ribs for Fritzie.

What do you think of Russia. The rotters have left us in the muck, they are worse than our strike leaders. Never mind Wait till the 'Yanks' start. According to their guessing etc they intend to finish the busness when they start. They can't beat our boys anyhow & they take care to keep their guessing to themselves when any are about. Half a dozen got poking muck at one of our infantry boys & he bogged right in & mixed things up till they cleared out.

Well dear all since dinner I have had a walk in one of those country lanes you hear about, hedges on each side & trees spreading their branches right over the top forming an arch. Its the first walk I have had & of course I could not go far owing to the pins being a bit shaky. . .

How is everything doing in the little grey home in the Sunny South? You will be right amongst the hot weather by the time this reaches you I suppose. The sun actually shone twice this week over here. Its not quite so cold as it was in France this time last year, but I expect it will be snowing before Xmas. Well dears I will ring off now so share my best love & kisses & kiss the nipps for me. Bye Bye

from Loving Son & Bro
Jack XXXXXXXXXXX

December came and Jack reported that he was 'still going strong & feeling fit again, too fit in fact. . .which means a step closer to France and the mud'. Now installed at Hurdcott, he spoke of the various concert parties that entertained the patients:

Some are cheered & some counted out, but every one seems to take it in good part. Im hanged if I know why the people stick to the Australians for they soon let enyone who is on the stage know if they are not pleasing them.

Last night 4 girls came to give us a show & an old chap came to look after them. He was not supposed to be in the business but when the boys spotted him (a non starter) they started yelling. 'Come on Dad lets have a little bit of rag' etc.

The old chap smiled & said he was not attached to the concern, but they would not have anyone else sing before Dad had a try. So in the finish he said 'Well boys as you have axed me I will do my best.' He made a terrible mess of his songs but the mob cheered & clapped him on twice & it just about knocked all the wind out of him.

Then, on the eve of Christmas, came welcome news of a furlough and Jack headed for his second home in Skewen and his 'second mother', Mrs Harris.

> Skewen
> Wales
> 23-12-17

Dear Mother Dad Sis & Bro

here we are again & this time I'm writing from my second home. I might assure you that Im in for a grand time while here. The girls have all sorts of arrangements ready for action during the Xmas holidays.

Of course I am rather strange being amongst all these girls on my own, but am quite sure I will get over it very soon. They are cut up at their cousin being killed, but I am sure of having a good time just the same.

Thank you so much dears for sending the money over, for you know now that I can really enjoy myself before going back to the mud. Just before my leave came out I received a bundle of 24 letters & six of them were from home, so you can see dears I am answering six in one. . .

Well dears I expect after my furlough is over I will go into training & hit France a few weeks after. Something big is coming off & they say they will be sending everyone back. I don't mind admitting that I intended swinging the lead in Winter was over, but am afraid it cant be did. Fred is getting on very well & marked the same as me, so we will most likely hit the mud together.

Bye Bye for the present dears & please kiss the nips for me.
> Best love & kisses to all
> from Loving Son & Bro
> Jack

> Skewen
> Wales
> 29.12.17

Dear Mother Dad Sis & Bro.

here we are again still in Skewen & having the time of my life. My second home. Goodness what a Christmas Ive had turkey every day since

Tuesday & have been everywhere with the girls. There was fun & giggles under the mistletoe on Xmas day. A bit different to the mud last Xmas!

On Boxing day we had a group of 5 taken so you will have one soon after this letter. Cassie is next to me Beatie next to the other chap (Ben) & the girl in the centre is Ben's sister Annie. Ben is a munition worker & is not allowed in Karki. I know that would be Mum's first question. They are fine friends all of them & during the holidays have taken me everywhere. Up to date I have £10 left so you see it has not cost me much. They want to pay everything. Musical evenings gallore too, every one either plays or sings except me. Tonight Im taking Cassie & Beatie to '1 Days Leave', play.

Every night or I should say morning we get to bed after midnight & I am always up before dinner. The weather has been lovely. The girls took me walking in the mountains & it was like spring weather. Everything points to me having a good time so I don't know how I'm going to leave on next Wednesday. . .

Mrs H. is such a dear old soal. The girls told my fortune with cards & you should have heard the tale they put up on me. This is the nearest to home that I've ever been yet. At present I'm in the kitchen (close to the fire). The cat is on my shoulder & the girls cleaning up. Its just 1 oclock & I've been up one hour.

By next Xmas dears I think we will be able to spend the holidays together. Things are very near an end now, but not quite as we would like them. Am so glad conscription was kicked back.

Well now dear all I must ring off again till next week. Give my best love to the nipps & kiss them both for me.

Bye Bye dears
with best love & kisses
from Son & Bro
Jack   XXXX   XXXX

Jack's mention of conscription referred to the second referendum on the subject, which was held in Australia on 20 December 1917. It was as bitter and nationally divisive as the first one, with the same result. Military conscription was rejected by 1,181,747 votes to 1,075, 199. The soldiers again favoured conscription but by a slightly reduced majority: Yes votes totalled 103,789 to 93,910 No votes. Gunner Duffell was eligible to vote this time, recording a resounding 'No'.

On his return to Hurdcott at the end of December, Jack wrote again about the warmth and friendship of the Harris family and their friends:

The musical evenings were just like old times. What I liked most was to get round the piano with Ben & the girls & run through the song books singing everything as it came along.

They all intend having a trip to Ausie after the war, especially Ben. He wanted to enlist once to see the business, but they would not let him leave the foundry work. He may be called up when the next order comes through. He is such a good chap Mum I know you would like him. He thinks the world of his Mother & Sister.

You should have seen the two of us on Xmas eve buying presents for the girls. It was the first time Ben had taken on the job of buying for ladies so you can guess the time we had especially as everyone had to have a look at me and wonder if I was a Yank or a cowboy.

After a few hours running after shop walkers etc we started home armed with the spoil Ben had a nice pair of framed pictures for his Mum & I had some boxes of the best linen handkerchiefs for the girls, and a bosker little table centre for the old lady. I bought Ben a nice cigarette case full while he presented me with a case of cigars. I had quite a lot of cards sent to me.

On New Years Eve I went to an evening with Ben & met a lot more girls & young chaps who made things merry till earley in the morning. I started the New Year by walking arm in arm with five girls down an old village road at 1 AM. in the morning. Not a bad start is it? I guess it was a lot nicer than being out sending a greeting over to Fritz.

I expect to be out amongst it again in a few weeks & I may get another 'Blighty'. Am not anxious for another dose of gas though. At present I am feeling pretty right so perhaps its not going to effect me anymore. Hope not anyhow.

Well dear Mum I could not use all the money, so I had plenty. When I was leaving I gave Mrs H. seven pound to hold for me & I had three myself so you see they would not let me spend much. Ben insisted on paying most of the time when we took the girls out. I dared not ask the old lady to take any board. You made an impression of them with your letter Mum.

The year 1917 had ended and Gunner Duffell wondered what 1918 held in store for him.

14

The Depths of Despair

The Allies did not enjoy much success in 1917. By the year's end Russia had made an armistice, the Italian allies were regrouping their positions, and the French Army was still weak and the British had little to show after four months of fighting. But the Americans were beginning to arrive and their sheer weight of numbers, more than anything else, was to prove decisive in the end.

The first half of 1918 was to be a crucial stage of the war and there was Gunner Duffell incarcerated in an army convalescent camp in Wiltshire, England, far away from his army mates in France.

During the next seven months he wrote thirty-seven long letters to his family in Hurstville, and they are open to interpretation.

At first Jack himself believed in the optimism he expressed to Dear Mother Dad Sis & Bro about a quick recovery from the gassing. He sent regular reassurances: 'I'm feeling heaps better' . . . 'I'm feeling pretty right just now' . . . 'Am doing famously' . . . 'I'm feeling tip top myself' . . . and so on. But as the weeks and months went by, with regular examinations by doctors, he began to realise that his condition was more serious than he had first thought. A gradual change in mood is discernible in his letters home. He kept telling his family that he would soon be back with his mates at the front, but one doubts if they were fooled.

A trace of bitterness appeared in his letters. His youthful cockiness seemed subdued and the inaction and boredom of camp life made him moody. Seeking diversion he managed to engage himself in a few army 'lurks'. He got a job as 'offsider' to the camp barber, lathering the 'wire beards' of those willing to pay threepence for a shave and sweeping up the clippings of the 'wild mops' of the sixpenny haircut patrons. The troops gave the barber and his offsider tips of money instead of using chits from the orderly room. 'Of course, strictly obeying camp regulations, we should not have handled any money,' Jack wrote. 'But being Diggers, regulations meant nothing except when we were in the line.'

Jack also did a stint as a cook's offsider, which provided him with much richer food than the ordinary camp patients enjoyed. He rebelled angrily, however, when detailed as a mess orderly to wash up dishes and serve the officers' mess—'young puppies who are no better than yourself', he termed them, little dreaming that in a later war he would be commissioned as an army captain himself.

Meantime, he was short-winded, prone to dizzy turns and constant headaches. If he went to see a film (he delighted in Charlie Chaplin) his head would ache for a week. He could not look out from a moving train without dizziness. His heart was subject to sudden stabs of pain.

On the brighter side, Gunner Duffell's opportunities and facilities for letter-writing had boomed. Pen and ink and writing paper were readily available from the Australian Red Cross and the YMCA at the camp. The letters flowed from him in a torrent. In addition to his letters home, he wrote hundreds to relatives, friends and girls. Throwing caution to the winds of nearby Salisbury Plains, he corresponded recklessly with up to twenty-seven girls, confessing to his mother that the outcome would probably be calamitous. A thing to be noted was that his handwriting and spelling improved markedly during this rash of correspondence.

Jack's burning desire to be back with the guns in France slowly changed to a desperate need to be returned to Australia. Another gas victim in the camp in a similar state of mind cut his throat, but Jack had no intention taking that way out. However, late in March, when he was marked 'unfit for active service for six months, with home service in England', Jack sank into the depths of despair and despondency at being so classified—a 'dud', he called himself miserably.

This mood coincided with bad war news from France and it further darkened Jack's depression. The Germans suddenly launched a powerful offensive. Their armies rolled across old Somme battlefields and threatened to break through where the British and French armies joined. The advance took them to within sixty kilometres of Paris before the Allied forces, responding to a dramatic 'backs to the wall' appeal by Field Marshal Haig, halted the enemy's momentum. It was a last-ditch effort by the Germans. The Australians performed with rare courage and determination at Villers-Bretonneux and other vital actions, but Gunner Duffell was not with them. It hurt him beyond description.

Jack applied twice in April for a return to active service or a discharge and a return to Australia but without success. He and other similar patients were examined fortnightly by a board of doctors who 'admired his spirit' but in May marked him for 'permanent light duty in England'.

The only bright spot for Jack was his 'second home in Wales'. The old jolly, cocky little Gunner Duffell surfaced again when he went on leaves. One suspects that 'dear old soal', Mrs Harris, recognised that he was simply a homesick young soldier of twenty, needing support and affection. The Harris family gave him plenty of both.

Early in June Jack Duffell was marked 'home for further treatment' and later in the month for 'return to Australia'. He was transferred to Westham Camp in Dorset and extracts from his letters home in this period mirror Jack's mental torture of not being able to rejoin his gunner mates at the front and the fear that he would be regarded as being 'cold-footed'. They also give vent to twin obsessions about the evils of conscription and what he considered to be the poor qualities of the English soldier. He kept writing on these subjects over and over again to his parents.

The subject of Gunner Duffell's opinion of the Tommy is a matter for debate. He may not have been aware or understood that England had lost the flower of its youth under the voluntary system, a whole generation wiped out before conscription was adopted and troops from other countries arrived on the scene. It should be noted that in his Postscript he adopted a much more temperate attitude towards the Tommies, though deploring the fact that the Australians always seemed to be the ones to be flung in as shock troops when the going was hard.

Jack blamed everything on conscription, conscript soldiers, conscript women, conscript nations. He wrote impassioned letters about it to his mother and father, who had both voted Yes in the Australian conscription referendums. His bitterness and intolerance may have reflected a dark desire to take it out on others as well as himself. Time would soften his cynicism, but the letters speak for themselves:

[13-1-18] . . .you did not like the idea of those men swinging it (pretending to be unfit) last winter I see. I am quite sure I did not blaim them & I intend doing the same thing myself. It does not make any difference to the men in France for they are reinforced by the fresh blood just over I have taken a tumble to being a 'good' soldier for the heads think no more of the stickers than any one else. Am just beginning to find out

that certain people are feathering their nests at the soldiers expense. At present I am here for the benefit of Australia & my people. Nothing else. I would not give a hang if Fritz took the whole of France & Belgium too. They are a rotten race all of them.

[20-1-18] I'm thinking that Fritz will make a determined offensive when the weather breaks & the Aussies will have to bear the brunt of it. They always put us in to do anything that the tommies fail at & up to date the boys have always done what they went in to do. I've seen our Infantry stand up to a barrage that twice the number of tommies have run from. Its the artillery that holds the line mostly when the tommies are in. When we covered them in July and August we had to answer SOS signals all night & every night. They won't stand & fight like the Ausie.

[2-2-18] I'm not doing too bad for friends eh? especially girls. Am only writing to five in Blighty & about 25 in Australia. Oh what a gay old time is coming someday. I often wonder if I will catch one out of the lot, for you know dears I am old enough to think about those things now.

I wonder if it will be an Ausie or a Welch girl. You know we get ten days marriage leave from here, so I might be tempted to get leave that way if they wont grant it any other way. I put in an application for four days leave a week back, but was turned completely down. Can just picture you all if you received a letter saying that I had tied the knot with a Welch girl. Don't think there is much chance of it happening though. It could be done though.

[7-2-18] I have not heard anything about the Military Medal, most likely it has not been granted. The stripe too had to be taken down when I reached England for I had not held it long enough to be gazetted full Bombadier before becoming a casualty. Never mind they can keep their stripes & medals too when I can be in Blighty & Wales.

[10-2-18] I smile at your remarks re conscription Mum, but I hope you have changed your views now that you know the soldiers know best. I quite agree about the cold foot mob but we don't want to give our country into the hands of the men who have mucked England up and who are anxious to do the same to our 'Aussie'. Its not worth it Mum just to catch a few cold feet who are not worth a second thought.

Do you know that once conscription got a hand we would never be our own *Masters* again? Conscription won't better the men over here. Hughes will have to make himself scarce when the boys get home. Don't let him kid to you...

We have a lot of tame huns running about the camp and daubing red paint over everything that a man is likely to rub against. They are pretty civil to the Australians though, wonder what would happen if they spat at us like they sometimes do to their Tommy guards. I wish they would (not killed a hun for a long while).

In one of his private letters to his father, dated 15 February, Jack was unusually frank about his medical condition:

Am still convalescent Dad but going strong. The old heart was hit to leg, you know & it is taking some time to get a natural stroke going. The wind is not too good now but I expect it will right itself some day.

The damn gas has mucked hundreds of men up, it effects a fellow in many ways & has got all the quacks thinking. Every man is effected differently. Some are almost blind others deaf and dozens have crook hearts. For 3 months or more I have seldom been without a headache but its all in the joke I suppose so I must not go crook. I don't like squeaking about my troubles Dad, but i Know you would rather know the truth. It will all come right though before long, so don't go getting worried, and dont let Mum worry, for I will no doubt be well on the road for another go by the time this reaches you.

[17-2-18] Well dears, I can say that I am feeling heapes better this last few days, than I have all along. The headaches have left me I believe, so when the old heart gets well I will be as right as rain again.

Perhaps I will have to take a hand in the beginning of the spring offensive after all and I was kidding myself that I would miss that little lot. Anyhow we won't worry over it till it comes 'eh?'.

[20-2-18] What an afternoon Ive had! Letters from every one, and in most cases from my girls. Oh dear they have all gone serious at once and are anxiously awaiting my return. Guess Ill want a division of 'Aussies' to protect me when the landing comes off.

[28-2-18] Oh Gee wouldent I like to hear Mum blowing the Anti Conscriptionists up. All the same I hope it never gets a hold in Australia. I know dears that you think it would help us but for all the good we would get out of conscription the country would bring 3 times the harm, for once conscription gets a hold, the country begins to suffer. Look at England France & every other conscripted country, all ground down under the iron heel.

We are in the 'heads' power enough now without being bound down after the war too. Take no notice of wounded men's talk. I expect the're afraid to talk against it when they get back because most people think they are turning on their mates. I did not mean to write all this, but like Mum I don't know when to stop when I start conscription talk.

In one letter he wrote sadly about his mate, Jack Harris, and the grief in the Welsh family when he was killed.

You know Jack and I used to look each other up after every one left on his signalling staff & I was the last gunner in old D Sub. We said then its a cert that one of us will go west yet, wonder who it will be.

Jack said he wanted go right out when his turn came. 'No lingering stunts for mine' he said.

Poor fellow he got his wish.

[3-3-18] Have just been reading of the rough doings Billee Hughes is getting. Why the blighter says that all the voters against conscription are Germans. Why the boys will hang him, let alone sling eggs at the rotter. [Eggs were thrown at Prime Minister Hughes at a referendum campaign rally at Warwick, Queensland in November, 1917.] Does he think that all of us that voted against his money making swindle are huns? I am a hun at that rate, and I assure you I'll give any of the boys a hand to string him up, later on.

Reinforcements won't bring us any more rests. The whole trouble is— The Australian troops have been doing most of the heavy fighting for some time and now most of the boys are dead. They want to conscript more so as to be able to send us in the heavy stuff, till every one is wiped out. Our five divisions are doing more than any Tommy ten now, and yet Hughes and his mob want to bring conscription upon the country that has done more than its share now.

You don't realise what happens in a conscripted country so for goodness sake vote against it if there is a next time or not at all. There now. I've got away from myself again. Don't know what everyone will think of me but I blow them all up over the conscription question.

[10-3-18] Will tell you of a rather funny affair that happened yesterday. One of the boys from the hut went to a play in a fairly large town on the plains here. About a dozen Tommy one star artists reserved the front seats. They were rather merry and as the play went on made themselves an annoyance by calling out to the various actors etc. They made it that hot that one girl broke down & left the stage, so the stage manager asked them to leave the place but they abused him till the people cried 'turn them out'.

The stage manager asked for a senior officer to order the young cubs out but no senior would take on the job. Well an 'Aussie' private jumped up and said 'is there any Aussies here?' about eighteen of the boys hopped up and the first digger said 'how about chucking the ??? out?, we're not going to have the play spoiled by them?' They got to business and after a bit of trouble emptied them out & chucked their coats, hats, stick etc after them amid great cheering from the people No wonder the diggers get on well eh?

[17-3-18] . . . letter from Mary Dircks with a copy of the Honour Board from the school. They have spelt the name in their own way I see. I guess Mary must be a pleasant girl she writes great letters.

[27-3-18] On Friday I set out for Wales and blew in at my second home about 9 p.m. Found them all well & was right away made welcome. They seemed more pleased than I did, when I mentioned being boarded for six months home service. On Saturday they packed me off to the sea side with Ben & after having a grand day we landed home and had some music. Sunday of course was spent in walks and church & another nice long stroll in the evening.

[31-3-18] I hope the four boys will come through OK from the heavy fighting that going on now. I'm lucky to be out of it, but I've a feeling that I ought to be in it. You know this will be the first big stunt that I've missed since the Aussie artillery came to France & when my Blighty came I didnt think it was going to knock me out for so long.

[3-3-18] Fancy Mrs Andrew crying over one of my letters. I don't want people to cry that way, the boys up in the line always manage to raise a LAUGH even during the hottest stunts. So you wont cry dear Mum will you?

[&-4-18] I do hope Dad is well again and able to work. If not I'm going to apply for my discharge or a trip home, because if I'm no use in France I want to get back & look after you all . . .

I don't want you to think I've got the wind up & am afraid to go back to the boys. I wouldnt mention it only I dont want to hang out in this country if I'm a dud as far as action is concerned.

The battle raged in France during April as the Allies fought to stem the German tide.

[14-4-18] The fit men are being rushed out and the old hands sent over to the line. The camp now is mainly composed of Duds like myself. Suppose I ought to thank my lucky stars that I'm not mixed up in the picnic over the other side but somehow I'm more discontented now than

I was in France... A fellow feels that he ought to be back with his cobbers. Camp mates are different to mates in action, where everyone works together & help one another.

[24-4-18] I intend putting an application in to be sent home. I'm not getting cold feet you know dears, but I'm not going to hang about in a dead & alive camp in this God forsaken country now that I'm a dud.

[27-4-18] I've sent my application in for a trip home as I think dears that would be a sure cure for me. No doubt some peole will sling off regarding cold feet etc but please remember anyone who does & perhaps I'll prove that they are wrong (in my own way). Don't suppose anyone will consider my application, but I want to know which way I'm going, Ausie or France...

With plenty of time on his hands, Jack approached the subject of matrimony should he, in fact, ever return to Australia, which seemed most unlikely to him at the time:

[19-5-18] Well Mother dear you took my jokes about getting married to heart didn't you? I've given the matter a good deal of thought lately & you may rest assured that Son Johney isn't going to tie himself up just yet. Yes Mum it would be rather hard on you to have to share your son with another.

I'm afraid the Johney you knew has vanished & an older one taken his place. I've changed my ways & views a terrible lot (not for the worse though) but I have still sense enough to take my parents advice. You don't like You-Know-Who Mum but she has never seemed anything but nice to me & I like her as much as any other girl, so we won't say any more about the matter.

I've not lost my heart to any girl yet Mum so don't worry that dear old head over those matters. Just listen to anything they have to tell you, but dont argue with them or you may bowl me out. I'm having the time of my life just finding out the good & bad points in all of them. I'm not troubleing my head how I'm going to get out of it on reaching home yet, thats a pleasure to come. Whats the use of being serious, I must do some mad things now & then or I'd become a man too soon.

Not a bad idea of yours Dad about coming home disguised but I'd rather see the fun on the wharf when the different girls turn up. Be a good stunt to give them a hat pin each & I take the winner. Guess there would be a hell of a mess though if they all turned on yours truly.

Then Jack was off again on his pet subject of conscript Tommy soldiers, apparently stung by the published remarks of an English officer to the effect that Australian soldiers were an 'undisciplined crowd of colonials, boastful and arrogant':

I see you have given me your views on conscription Dad & I must admit some of them sound O.K. but you only speak of those skunks who kicked up the strike etc.

It would be no use sending conscripts over here because they would only turn round & run like the conscripted Tommies do. You cant be expected to know what conscription means because you havent seen the result of it. Perhaps if you had half an idea of the state France & this country is in through it you would change your views on the spot.

I can truthfully say that I'd willingly go over to the line & 'go West' than see Australia in the hands of the conscriptionists. Do you know they are talking of conscripting women now? God its awful to think women may be called up like so many sheep & sent on any job they choose to bung them into. If the Tommies had any guts they would kick against the question.

Our boys who are coming over from France from the latest stunts say Fritz just makes a stunt against the Tommies when ever he likes & always goes through. They are putting French & Aust. & Canadian troops amongst the Tommy regiments with orders to shoot on anyone attempting to leave the line before being ordered.

An officer was telling us that our boys were holding a village on the Somme, but every man was in the line except cooks. This Officer wanted to get some tucker up to our boys, so he just walked about & rounded up half a dozen Tommies, who were supposed to be lost (having bunked) & told them to pick up the dixies & follow him to the line. He promised to shoot any one who tried to run.

Now what do you think of conscripts? Can't see why returned men should be looking for work. Surely the places of all the men over here are not filled up with pommies. You did what you thought was best tho Dad so let us drop it at that, but in the event of another referendum think it over before you vote more of our men in to do the work of the *brave* Tommy.

June came and the news was brighter on all fronts, including that of Gunner Duffell. The Allies were at last beginning to push back the Germans. The Australians and Americans had combined for the first time to capture the important sector of Hamel on 30 May. There was a new air of confidence at the front.

And Gunner Duffell at last was classified for 'return to Australia for further treatment'. He was transferred to Westham Camp in Dorset, about a twenty-minute walk from the Channel port of Weymouth. Jack greeted the news with mixed feelings, 'overjoyed' to be going home to Hurstville, downcast at not being able to be with his mates in what might develop into the final victory 'stunt':

Weymouth
England
16.6.18

Dear Mother Dad Sis & Bro,

another Sunday on hand so I'm on the job. No need to say I'm still in England & how anxious I am to be underway for the good old 'home sweet home'.

We are still waiting in the boat camp for our ship which is expected to come to light any day. I'm writing just the same in case the unforseen happens & I'm disappointed.

The old heart is behaving better lately & headaches are getting 'Tres Bein'. Hope you are all in the pink at the little Grey Home & getting a good old smile going for when the boy lands in kicking up a row. . .

I've had the luck to be seeing the sights etc in company with a nice little girl. She is in service down here & doesn't get out as much as I'd like but she is a real deacent & quiet 'Dorset' lassie. I laugh at the twang all the time I'm out with her. Dont let the cat out though Mum to all my 'Aussie' girls for I must catch one out of that little lot if I land back. You know a fellow must have company. I reckon I'm lucky in finding such a 'Pal' 'Hum La!!!?'

Well dears I must ring off for the present & I trust that by next Sunday to be on the water. Remember me to all the friends please & share by best love & kisses between you.

Bye Bye for the present again. Love & kisses to all

from your Loving Son & Bro
Jack   XXXX
XXXX

15

End of a Perfect Day

It was nearly a month before a repatriation ship became available. Jack 'walked out' with his little Dorset girl and, for variety, was involved in a riot between Australian soldiers and American sailors. Jack reported that military police, called in to quell the disturbance, were badly beaten up by both sides and the Diggers won the fight.

At last the day came. Jack and 600 other war wrecks, as he called them, entrained at Weymouth for Plymouth, where the SS *Barunga* awaited them at the docks. The ship was towed out into the stream and anchored not far from Nelson's historic ship, *Victory*. Jack wondered what Nelson would think of this war of the twentieth century.

The *Barunga* took to sea and by dark steamed past the lighthouse at Lands End. Soon the shores of England faded into the darkness and half a world away lay Australia. But the Germans had not quite finished with Gunner Duffell. Three days later he was back at Weymouth with 600 others, while the *Barunga* was at the bottom of the Bay of Biscay.

Weymouth
England
17.7.18

Dear Mother Dad Sis & Bro

about the time this reaches you I should have arrived back, but Fritz hadn't finished with the boy so I'm back in England again. Made a start on Sunday the 14th & went 300 miles or so when up popped a sub & jammed a torpedo into our old hooker. He missed the engine room as luck would have it & tore half our starboard side away between the engine room & bow.

Great joke (don't think) jumping into the atlantic ocean but it had to be did. We had four nurses & some bad chaps aboard & of course they were swung over in the boats, but the rest of us had to take to the water & be picked up by the boats after the destroyers had taken the nurses etc aboard.

We were all taken on destroyers after Fritz had been fixed up & sailed back to old 'Blighty' at 27 notts.

Our ship was one of the hun boats captured from the outbreak of war, but it was her first & last attempt as a troopship. I hear we are the first load of returning 'Aussies' to be torpedoed, but now its all over I wouldn't have missed it for quids. Everyone kept cool & as far as I can hear no lives were lost.

The boys went over in good order & a few at a time. The heavy swell prevented the life boats coming alongside so we had to swim out. Many took to the rafts & waited till everyone came from the ship & then they struck out for the destroyer.

You could see about half a dozen on a raft hanging on & singing or cracking jokes at the swimers etc. One mob were singing 'This is the end of a perfect day' It was about 5 in the evening so they were about right.

We got into dry stuff about 20 hours after being struck & you should have seen us coming off in our dry clobber, some in sailors rig others in Tommy & several with civey stuff. I managed to grab a pair of long pants, a pair of canvas shoes & a shirt. I hung to my tunic & dried it as I went along. Have all 'Aussie' stuff again now though as they fitted us up this afternoon.

We came back to our own camp & expect to have another try in a few weeks time.

Its getting too dark to write any more so I'll have to close. Excuse Pencil but I lost everything except my pocket book & Bible from the church. The belt of badges went money belt, pen & lots of little things I wanted to take back. Best of love to you all from Son & Bro. Jack X X X X

The detailed account of the sinking of the *Barunga* written by Jack Duffell over two decades later, is worth reproducing in full:

Dawn next morning found most of the troops lining the rails & admiring the 3 escorting destroyers & the cruiser, Kent who was going along with us with its own escorting destroyers.

All day we steamed into the Bay of Biscay & the sea took on that heavy swell so noted there. Late in the afternoon a light rain began to fall. At several points about the ship guards were posted, their duty being to watch the sea in case of a submarine attack. A gun crew composed of Aussie naval men (who were returning to Australia on long service leave) stood by the 4 inch gun mounted at the stern of the Barunga.

My cobber Roy was up forward on deck yarning to me when the bugle blew for tea & as I was feeling a bit off colour Roy volunteered to bring my mug of tea etc on deck to me.

He was gone only a few minutes when a guard shouted 'Look out Sub?' A second later a tearing crash & the deck under my feet lifted & I was thrown onto my hands & knees. A great volume of greenish yellow smoke rose from the side of the ship opposite to where I was sprawling.

Rushing across the deck I saw what had happened. A gaping hole some 12 feet wide was torn in the great iron plates & it extended well below the water line. Boxes & bales were swirling out & a horrible sucking rumbling was going on beneath the deck at my feet.

A torpedo had struck us in the forward hold just in front of the engine room & the ship at once began to dip at the bow. The only glimpse I had of the sub was as it dived towards & under the 'Barunga'. Boat stations were blown & the troops quietly fell in by the boats on rafts. Life belts were donned by all hands.

The more severely wounded & the nurses were helped into the boats & lowered away. At the same time rafts were thrown over board & men began to take to the water, some used knotted ropes that hung over the side at various intervals. Others just jumped for it. Soon the sea was dotted with life boats & rafts that rose & dipped at the swell of the huge waves.

The old 'Barunga' was doomed & had developed a distinct list to port & was settling deeply nose first. Very little had been seen of the submarine as it dived toward & under the 'Barunga' soon as the torpedo struck. My only glimpse was a rusty grey shape disappearing into the depths.

The naval detachment fired one shot but they had little hope of a hit. The cruiser 'Kent' sent out a smoke screen & made off towards the French coast 200 miles away, while the 3 destroyers, Lance, Midge & Victory raced round the sinking ship dropping depth charges. These depth charges exploded beneath the water with a terrific roar & sent columns of black smoke & water high into the air.

Stopping a ships officer I asked how far we were from land? Pointing over his left shoulder he said 'Two hundred miles that way' & then pointing to his feet, 'two miles that way'.

I thanked him. He also mentioned that two bulkheads were holding the ship afloat for the present but she would sink like a stone when they went. I wondered just how long will they hold.

By this time one of the destroyers had hove to & was taking the wounded from some of the life boats & these boats began picking the swimmers from the water, while others came alongside the 'Barunga' & took off those who were lucky enough to jump in. This was not easy as the huge waves of the Bay of Biscay were running true to form & half the time the boats were afar beyond jumping distance & many of the troops dropped into the sea.

My kit bag was below deck in a rack above the mess table so I decided to get it as it contained several things I wanted to have before abandoning the ship. Making my way to the stairs leading below I was amazed at the lack of confusion as noone seemed perturbed & many were joking over the situation.

It did not take me long to find my kit & as soon as possible I was back on deck as I did not like the idea of the ship taking the final plunge while I was below deck. Selecting a few small items that fitted into my tunic pockets I began making preparations for taking to the water. It was a case of take to the water I knew as I had delayed too long & the raft I had been allotted with some others had been thrown over some time before.

Roy, my mate found me & said he was going over & intended swimming out to the destroyer that was hove too about 200 yards away. Owing to my heart condition I was not keen to take on a swim of that distance so I told him I would hang on awhile in the hopes of getting into one of the life boats. He stayed by my side like the cobber he was & I knew he intended to stick on hand in case I had one of my old heart turns.

A few of us broke open the dry canteen & we helped ourselves to cigarettes, chocolate, biscuits etc. As it seemed a long time since lunch & perhaps a lot longer to the next meal I opened a tin of preserved pineapple & together with a dozen biscuits it made a good tea. Roy called me several kinds of a fool for eating when having to take to the water probably.

One incident of the many happening, stuck into my mind above all others. A band sergeant noted for his ability with the cornet, stood looking over the side. He still held the silver cornet he had won during a competition in England. We had heard him play often.

Presently he turned & said 'I'm going to play one last tune on her anyhow', & climbing upon the raised hatch he played 'The end of a perfect day'. All eyes were turned towards him & as the notes of that old song floated out over the hectic scene mine & the thoughts of a few hundred others are better imagined than described.

As the last note died away Sergeant Ted Hunter tossed his cornet far out over the side & it disappeared on its long wet journey to the depths of the Biscay. The last I saw of the player he was going down a knotted rope to join the many others who were being tossed about in the sea.

My boots were discarded & I waited by the rail awaiting the chance to jump into a boat. Two destroyers still raced round & the roar of depth charges told us that the sub had not been sunk & at any moment it might pop up & slam another torpedo into the stricken Barunga or perhaps into the destroyer that was picking up the troops. A sitting shot.

Presently there was a terrible crash & tearing deep down below decks of the 'Barunga'. Roy shouted 'Thats another bulk head gone' & to prove it the ship took a sudden & deeper list. By this time about ⅓ of the forward portion was under water & it was difficult to stand even by hanging onto the ships rails.

Roy said 'I'm going over Gunner' (I was known to the boys as gunner) He went over the side & I watched him clear the ships side & strike out for the destroyer. As I still held back he looked up & shouted 'Come on gunner you will have to get wet'.

There didn't seem any chance of getting into a boat & as the ship might go at any moment now I tossed aside the few clothes I had hoped to take with me & climbed through the rails. By the aid of a knotted rope I went hand over hand at the same time trying to steady myself against the rolling of the ship.

Reaching the end of the rope I looked down at the dark water. Ugh, it looked deep & cold & as I looked the ship rolled over & the water dropped away. The thought flashed through my mind she was turning over & I was hanging there like the weight on the end of a plumbob. In fear I let go & dropped down, down & splash.

It seemed an age before I came to the surface & there was the red & rusty plates of the Barunga above me & she was rolling back again towards me. Seemed that I would be crushed under those steel plates with several others close by me, but although scared to death I was not hurt by banging against the ship.

In the excitement I forgot about my bad heart & endevoured to kick my way from the ships side. This was not easy & wave after wave washed me back. One moment I was almost level with the deck of the ship & the next as she rolled away I was underneath the keel.

I had experienced 'wind up' in action often enough but it was nothing to how I felt for that few minutes till at last I got away on a receeding wave & was swimming away towards the destroyer. One moment while on the top of a huge wave I could see everything for miles round but the next would be down in the trough & seemed all alone in that huge Bay of Biscay.

The life belt kept me afloat but trying to swim up the sides of waves was like trying to climb a brick wall. Roy had disappeared amongst the many who like us were bobing about like corks in a tub of stirred up water.

One of the destroyers dashed past & a great oil drum arrangement shot into the air & landed in the sea. I knew it was a depth charge & waited on the discharge. Bang it went & although some few hundreds of yards away I felt the jar & something like an electric shock passed through my frame.

Several charges burst in quick succession away astern of the 'Barunga' & although I did not know it, the Destroyers had located the U boat & were concentrating on the position.

While on the crest of a wave I saw one of the life boats quite close to me & the next wave brought me along side. Helping hands pulled me into the boat & I was sprawled into the foot or so of water in the bottom of the boat. Several other half drowned objects were in the boat which was manned by sailors.

Helped drag half a dozen other Diggers from the sea & then we set out for the destroyer I had been trying to swim to. On reaching the rolling side it proved most difficult to get aboard. We just had to jump for it each time the deck & the life boat reached the same level. A naval officer caught my arm as I jumped & I was pushed out of the way to make room for the next man. As the small craft rolled I fell over someone on the deck & soon someone fell over me & there I stayed & watched the work of rescue.

A cheer went up from one of the Destroyers half a mile astern of us & we guessed they had skittled the submarine. Soon one of the Destroyers raced up & began taking men out of the water while the third destroyer continued steaming round the scene & she was our guard in case another sub put in an appearance.

The poor old 'Barunga' was a sorry sight, & by this time all hands had left her. Standing almost on her nose she was cracking her back. It is an unforgettable sight to see a good ship slowly sinking & the weird noises that issued from the stricken vessel will remain with me always.

At last after about 2 hours since the bursting of the torpedo all hands had been picked up & the two destroyers leapt to life & swung away from the 'Barunga'. As we pulled away the other Destroyer ceased to circle. She steamed past the 'Barunga' & a gun roared & the shell stuck the doomed ship at the water line right where her back was breaking.

They were sinking her as quickly as possible & making sure that no derelect wreck would be left to menace other shipping. A sailor told me that sometimes a sinking ship would become waterlogged & float just below the surface for days, so the navy saw to it that the 'Barunga' went well down. I thought of the two miles to the bottom & wondered how long it would take her to make the journey.

Well that was that, & instead of being well on my way to Australia on that old ship she was slipping down into the deep & I was packed like a sardine on a naval craft that was plowing back to England at about 27 knots.

She carried about 300 other sardines besides myself & as her normal crew was about 70 not much space was left unoccupied by a wet & half dead khaki clad Digger.

Darkness closed the scene & except for the dark wall of water racing past each side of the little craft nothing much else was to be seen. There were no lights on the destroyer & it was cold as sin lying there soaking wet & a cold wind blowing. Before leaving the 'Barunga' I had filled one of my tunic pockets with cigarettes & chocolates & although at that moment I would have sold my soal for a smoke my pocket was now full of a sodden mush of cigarettes & choc well mixed. Anyhow it was worth more than a mans life to light a match with the eagle eyed naval officers present.

Those closest to the sailors quarters were lucky enough to share in dry clothes & the food the good natured tars passed round. Being one of the last picked up I was well out in the cold & missed everything but the icy wind.

Sometime during the night I heard a familiar voice. It was Roy who I had last seen from the deck of 'Barunga'. He was crawling round amongst the troops now asking if 'Any of you cows seen my cobber Gunner?'

Wasn't I pleased to hear that son of a gun again. 'Over here boy I called & soon he was by my side & we were good naturedly abusing each other which was usual when we met in any unusual circumstances. He had some tobacco which had remained dry in an oil silk pouch & I chewed a wad of that while he unfolded a plan to get down to the stoke hold & dry off. Telling him to lead off I followed his feet as he crawled over the cursing troops & out along the pitching deck where a small round hatch came to view.

This Roy raised & I followed him down an iron ladder into the oil burning stoke hold. What a difference, here was warmth & I needed it. Roy informed me that he had been down there before & decided to find me if possible as he guessed I'd be wet & not feeling the best.

The reason Roy knew his way about a destroyer was owing to the fact that the Father of a girl he had palled up with in England, commanded Destroyers & Roy had been shown over one. The fact stood to us & soon I was warm again & watched the navy boys burn oil by the means of turning on a tap. What a difference to the old method of shovelling coal into a furnace. We were informed that the three destroyers were the 'Midge' 'Lance' & Victory & the one we were on was the Midge & the other two were somewhere close by, tearing back to England.

By daylight our clothes were dry so Roy & I crawled back to the deck where we found most of the troops trying to infuse some life into cramped legs & arms. Nearing the English coast we passed other ships & the crews stared at the unusual sight of Destroyers packed with soldiers.

At 10 AM Tuesday 16th July our little ship slid up to a pier at Plymouth & we all streamed ashore & after sending up three hearty cheers for the sailors who had rescued us, we formed up & marched off to a huge mess room at the barracks & there were fed up on hot soup & thick slices of bread.

This meal was the first since lunch on the Barunga 15 hours back. The way those 'Tars' shared out smokes etc to us besides dry underclothing socks etc proved the good fellows they were.

A train was made available & by 2 PM we were crammed aboard & on our way back to Weymouth. That same night at 8.30 we left the train & there on the platform were greeted by thousands of Diggers & citizens of Weymouth. My little Dorset girl was there which was the one redeeming feature of the whole disaster.

Ambulances carried us back to Westham camp where another welcome awaited us & the Y.M.C.A. & Salvation Army organisations gave free house which enabled us to stock up with lots of small items we needed. Bed was welcome to most of us soon as it was possible to find one. Huts were allotted & once again we poor ship wrecked motly crew settled down to camp life.

16

Mary Dircks Gets her Man

While waiting for another ship, Jack was granted six days leave and of course headed straight for his 'second home' and 'second mother', who sent him £5 on learning that Jack's paybook had gone down with the *Barunga*.

It was a halcyon interlude. There were walks through the green valleys and hills of South Wales with Ben, Cassie and Beatie. And there were the 'feeds' of glorious food unobtainable in camp—white bread, real butter, bacon and eggs, ham and fish suppers.

'Well dears,' Jack wrote home, 'I'd get well in about a month if up here I think. You cant imagine how good everyone is.

'Since arriving I've been presented with a tip top fountain pen from the people & a watch from Ben so you can see what friends I've made. They are the finest people in the world bar none.'

Jack's parting with the Harris family was tearful, with all kinds of promises for reunions after the war. Cassie vowed that she would be going to Australia.

A week later the torpedoed troops entrained at Weymouth for Plymouth to join another ship bound for Australia, but both train and troops returned to Weymouth within the hour. The ship they were to have boarded had been sunk by a German submarine the night before while steaming into Plymouth. Several hours later they were in the train again, bound for Plymouth the second time and another ship, SS *Carpentaria*. This time luck was to be with them.

The *Carpentaria* was attached to an Atlantic convoy of twenty-three ships which steamed out to sea on 9 August 1918. There were three lines of them, escorted by ten destroyers, several seaplanes and an airship. On the following morning, the *Carpentaria* and three other ships left the main convoy and steamed off south, escorted by two destroyers.

Just before dark, one of the destroyers steamed in close to the *Carpentaria*. The troops lining the rails of their ship wondered what it was all about. Then a British sailor stood up on the bridge of the destroyer and slowly semaphored a message, 'Good luck and goodbye Lance'.

'What a cheer went up from our men,' Jack recalled. 'Again and again we cheered & the jack tars returned our cheers & then in a flash that grey little craft raced away with its mate & soon we were left without an escort.'

There were some uneasy minds aboard the *Carpentaria* that night but nothing happened except some good wireless news from France about an Allied victory. British and French troops had captured thousands of prisoners and 700 guns. It seemed to be the beginning of the end of the Germans.

The following day the *Carpentaria* left the three other ships and set off alone for the west coast of Africa. The doctors had warned Jack that excessive heat would be detrimental to his condition and so it proved to be. The approach of the tropics strained his heart and for days on end his head ached intolerably, any exertion bringing on a dizzy turn. He was not able to take any part in the crossing the line horseplay ceremonies.

The ship called at Sierra Leone and Cape Town before setting off across the Indian Ocean to Australia. The troops were granted leave at Cape Town and Jack reported that the 'last night finished up with a riot in the Opera House which was merry while it lasted & I got a beautiful thick ear'.

The news on the wireless continued to be good too, with further big advances by Allied troops. 'We were missing the best part of the war,' Jack wrote, 'but it was some satisfaction to know that I had done my bit in the period of the hardest fighting & the boys were making a good job of it to finish Fritz off.'

The voyage across the Indian Ocean was uneventful. Gunner Duffell wrote his one hundred and fifty-third and last letter home to Hurstville at sea two days before the *Carpentaria*'s arrival in Fremantle. One of his greatest concerns was how to cope with the number of girls he had dallied with by correspondence and he told his mother he thought he would need a bodyguard on arrival. What Jack did not know was that no bodyguard in the world would be able to prevent Mary Dircks from getting her man. For his part, he seemed to have narrowed the field down to a short list of three, Rhoda, Mary, and an Olga:

At Sea
25.9.18

Dear Mother Dad Sis & Bro

Although still a week from W.A. I must get a move on to have a letter ready for when the Wests go off.

I can't realise yet that I'm only a couple of days off that little Grey Home we have mentioned so often.

Goodness knows how many letters were lost lately as I know a couple of ships went south but no doubt at least one got through letting you know how our first attempt to reach home was stopped by Fritz with the aid of a torpedo. This time though the old Carpentaria brought us through safely up to date & Fritz paid no special attention.

Well dears you will no doubt be warned when we are due in Sydney but I'll wire from Melbourne if we have a pay between now and then. I hear we are going overland from Melbourne and I expect to get in a few days before my birthday. You may get your boy back after all Mum.

The food's getting a bit rough & I'm longing to taste the puddings Mother used to make etc. I suppose I needn't mention the fact that I dont want to see a stew for ages. Steak & eggs will do me for the first week but I know everything will be good if its left to Mum . . .

I've kept well in everyway except when in the tropics where the heat set the head aching for a week or so. Am feeling pretty well now except for the head which has taken one of the everyday aching stunts like it used to do in England. That isn't worrying me though dears so don't let it worry you. I'm thinking you will get a surprise to see me looking so well. Bit thin on it but nothing to what I'll pick up on decent living.

Am writing to Rhoda, Mary Dircks, Olga & Harry Hunt besides yourselves so bye bye for the present.

Best love & tons of kisses to all at the little grey home where I trust to be in a week's time.

Keep smiling
Your loving Son & Bro
Jack X X X X X X

All hands on the *Carpentaria* were up at dawn on Friday, 27 September, looking for their first sight of Australia. 'At 6 AM it was sighted & for a time there was a dead silence it seemed too good to be true,' Jack wrote:

For my part I remembered my feelings & thoughts as that same land had faded away from sight when I was on my way over at the end of 1915. I was seeing it again at the end of 1918 but under quite different circumstances.

The boys at last broke out & cheers for Australia & for the ships captain and for anything we thought worthy rent the air. The birds wheeling over head gave us welcome, but they must have thought us mad.

We were tied up to the Freemantle pier by lunch time, & there on the wharf were good old Australian people, mothers, fathers, sisters & brothers all the loved ones there to greet the West Australian portion of our war worn complement & did we cheer them all!

The rest of the 'war-worn' troops were granted four hours shore leave and given warm-hearted hospitality by the people of Fremantle. Jack could not help grinning at the contrast to his last visit to Fremantle with the *Berrima* boys and wondered what had happened to the 'rotter colonel'.

The *Carpentaria* steamed out again at 6 p.m., bound for Melbourne. The troops had received wide publicity as the survivors of a German torpedo attack and the brass bands were out in their honour:

The Victorian people extended a welcome equal to that given in West Australia & many gifts of smokes etc were showered on us as we marched from the ship to a waiting train that waited to take we N.S.W. men on the final stage to home. Amid cheers & the stiring strains of an old war march played by a brass band the train left for Albury. There we detrained & had a good tea at 9 p.m.

A red cross hospital train pulled in & each man was allotted a bed & soon we were over the border & in New South Wales. I did not sleep much as my thoughts of the new day when I would meet my loved ones did not permit sleep. At all the big stations people were waiting to welcome & cheer us on.

It seemed strange that men & women went to so much trouble to welcome men that they did not know, but we were fellow Australians & the war made us all Brothers & Sisters. We were war heros but many of us did not feel heros. Just a batch of maimed & broken men, not broken in spirit, but as soldiers we were of no further use to the country & were being laid aside. I suppose those people who came to us offering smokes & a gay word realized this.

At Moss Vale we had a good breakfast & then on again for Sydney. Soon old familiar landmarks were passed & to cheers & bands we slowly steamed into Sydney Station at 10 a.m. Oct 4th 1918.

By this time my heart was turning somersaults & my head was whirling. Excitement was not good for me, but who could be calm at a time like that. My memory of the next hour is just a jumble of one joy after another.

First I scaned the waiting crowd for my people & there were hundreds of faces to look over. At last I saw them, about 25 yards away. Mother, Dad & my young Sister & Brother, how the kids had grown. Mum was the first to get to me & then at the expense of a big policeman who thought a tornado had hit him as Mum dashed passed. I was in one of the many cars that was to take us to the Anzac Buffet in the Sydney Domain.

There was no time for much of a greeting at the moment but Dad managed to get through the barrier of police and as the car moved off he popped my young brother into the car & off it went with the young chap perched on my knee. He didn't know me of course as he was only 2 years old when I went away. We were soon cobbers though & as the cars slowly made way through the crowded streets my car came in for quite a bit of cheering & many packets of smokes due mostly to the little Digger (they thought) perched on my knee.

The fact that we were the torpedoed mob was known to that Sydney crowd & being the only boat load to receive that special attention from our old friend Fritz, our welcome was something out of the ordinary.

Strong posts comprising what seemed the pick of Sydney's pretty girls sang to us until we began to think we really had done something. Finally the gates of Sydney Domain were reached & as my car was about to pass through a tornado in the shape of two pretty girls landed on the running board & I was caught up in the arms of the girl who later became my wife. The other girl being her sister. Mary Dircks had knitted sox & corresponded with me for most of my war service but till that moment we had not met.

The business of brief medical examination & being issued with leave passes took about an hour & then I was free to meet my people who had a car waiting at the gates.

The excitement of it all proved more than the old heart could stand & the memory of that car ride to my old home at Hurstville remains a blank. I do know that during the next two days dozens of old friends & relations came to the place & with it all I felt like a fish out of water & cleared out for a few hours on my own to enable me to collect my scattered wits.

One gets used to anything in time & as the weeks sped past was able to adapt myself to the role of returned soldier. A few days after returning

I attained the age of 21 & mans estate. This fact gave me food for thought & I wondered what the future held for a war wreck.

During the early days of November rumours of Armistice negotiations filtered through & on the eleventh hour of the eleventh day of the eleventh month 1918 the last shot was fired & Germany was beaten. It went against the grain to be so far from the boys in the moment of Victory, but the calm which resulted after the first mad 24 hours showed that each one of us were busy with our own thoughts. Mine were, how was I to settle down to civil life again.

It was not until March 25 1919 that I was finally discharged as unfit for further service & once again gathered together clothes of a civilian & laid aside the uniform that I had known for three years 163 days, of which two years 294 days were spent overseas. Thus ended the service of one who served to the best of his ability.

17

Farmer Duffell

A civilian again, Jack Duffell lived at his parents' boarding house in Hurstville and looked around for a suitable peacetime occupation. He had been a packer with a wholesale firm, Gollans, before enlisting in the AIF but did not fancy that kind of job again. The Commonwealth Government was offering many repatriation training courses for 'returned soldiers', as they were called, and for some unknown reason Jack chose a course in upholstery.

In the meantime, he had fallen deeply in love with Mary Dircks, who he called Mollie. He did not have to woo her very hard, as she found the original of the wartime photograph very much to her liking. An accomplished young woman who had been dux of the Belmore Public School for every year of her attendance, Mollie was seven months older than Jack and lived in the nearby suburb of Belmore. A surviving notebook of his contains a long list of the train times from Hurstville, via Strathfield, to Belmore and return.

Jack did not take to upholstery to any great extent and neither did Mollie, who by then had eagerly accepted his proposal of marriage. Then the happy engaged couple became aware of the government's offer of unimproved land for discharged servicemen of the AIF in what was to become the Murrumbidgee Irrigation Area (MIA) of south-west New South Wales.

Irrigation water for the MIA first became available in 1913 after the completion of the Burrinjuck Reservoir, but the first five years were disastrous because of the settlers' ignorance of irrigation techniques, administration mistakes and other causes. Many settlers left their farms.

Settlement was revived, however, in 1919 with a government plan for ex-servicemen. Soldier settlers were offered £625 from the N.S.W. Water Conservation and Irrigation Commission to establish them as farmers. Rents and water rates would be suspended for two years on dairy farms and five years on horticultural holdings.

Jack and Mollie decided to make a break from the city to the country, not only for the prospects of rural fortune but for the benefit of Jack's mental and physical condition.

In order to qualify as settlers, the returned soldiers were obliged to work in gangs for up to a year preparing farms for ballot. This meant a long separation for the couple but they knew it would only be a postponement of their eventual marriage.

So, in 1920, Jack set off for Yenda, near the newly created towns of Leeton and Griffith, to hew out a home for his bride-to-be. The new settlers lived in barracks and tents. They toiled from dawn to dark under the most primitive conditions, clearing the thick scrub and undergrowth of an arid countryside. It was backbreaking work in the heat and dust and it is a wonder Jack's heart and legs stood up to it. As it was, John (as he was known there) Duffell was reckoned to be the hardest worker of them all. Few of them had any knowledge of irrigation farming, or any other kind of farming for that matter.

One of the diggers left this impression behind in a 1934 issue of *Reveille*, the RSL magazine:

There had been a drought in the Riverina for about two years and the whole place was being ravaged by a burning hot westerly that was a cross between a Saharan sirocco and a Nubian sandstorm.

Dry! Well, not only in the matter of nature's gentle precipitations was it lacking. While all the rest of the State outside its boundaries could quaff beer without stint, local prohibition was the rule. Not a very strict rule, it's true, but . . . Some men make their own hells, they say, and some have hell wished upon them, so I could not reasonably find anything wrong with the one I had personally selected.

Rough, she was, and tough, clearing the yarran, pine and box that clustered the ground. Hot she was, and dry. But there was on every hand a purposeful gathering of war veterans, all brimming with constructive ideals.

From every unit and from every front they had foregathered, drawn together once more by the clarion of strife, not for the purposes of wasteful warfare, but for the solid construction work of peace. Men of their hands, one and all, they were finding something very satisfying in the soul-stirring task of fighting nature, and making a sun-smitten wilderness blossom like a rose.

By the end of 1921, Jack had cleared enough land to qualify for a farm and had started to build a house. He and Mollie decided to wait no longer, even if they had to live in a tent for a while, and were married in Hurstville Methodist Church in December 1921. After a brief honeymoon, twenty-four year-old farmer Duffell carried his bride over the entrance to their canvas tent home on Farm 1348, Yenda.

In a way, it was a moment in history. The soldier settlers and their families were destined to help convert a desert into an Australian Garden of Eden. The MIA became known as an 'irrigation miracle of water into wine'. They had provided a base for what is now the most progressive and productive irrigation area of Australia—'Australia's rice bowl'. Yet hard times lay ahead.

By the end of 1921 most of the settlers were in occupation of farms of about fifteen to twenty acres (six to eight hectares) and preparing to plant trees and grape vines. Larger allotments of up to 150 acres (60 hectares) were being established as dairies and mixed farms. Sustenance payments to the men were taken into account when the 'charge upon the land' was apportioned to each farm and had to be repaid when they became productive. The Duffells were given a weekly sustenance of 32 shillings.

When the house was finished, they called it Gleneta. A battle lay ahead of them but they were both hard workers and very much in love. Their first son, Thomas John, was born at Yenda in October 1922. A second son, Roy, was born in March 1924, but he died tragically in December 1935 at the age of eleven. A daughter, Gwendalyn, was born in May 1928.

The Duffells prospered with their fruit and vines and were able to acquire two more farms over the next twenty years.

Many of the other soldier settlers were not so fortunate. Markets for their products became very limited and some had to find alternative work to survive. By 1928 the size of the farms had to be increased, which meant that one in three settlers were required to leave without reward for their years of effort and hardship. The Great Depression of the 1930s caused more of the soldier settlers and their families to walk off their small holdings, which were amalgamated with neighbouring farms. This was a sad blow after all their hard work and strivings.

Soldier settlers have not been forgotten, though, and nor have their sons and daughters who fought and died in World War II. During

Australia's bicentennial year in 1988, the citizens of Griffith decided to erect a memorial in honour of the soldier settlers and their children.

The Griffith Soldier Settlers Memorial was unveiled on 14 April 1990, 'in proud and honoured memory of some 2000 returned soldiers of the AIF who came to this area at the end of the Great War 1914–1918. The memorial also signifies the debt we owe to those of their sons, many of whom gave their lives during the World War of 1939–45.' The memorial depicts a World War I soldier with one hand resting on the handle of a single-furrow plough, and the other seen to be handing a service rifle to his son, clad in World War II battledress, who takes up arms for Australia as had his father before him. Many of the roads surrounding Griffith are named in honour of soldier settlers and parks of East Griffith are named in memory of their sons.

Farmer Duffell lived a full life at Yenda for a surprisingly long time, considering his disabilities. He never let on that he had any disabilities, although Mollie knew all about them. The mustard gas had left him with a chronically bad heart but doctors feared to give him a bypass operation because of the swollen veins in his discoloured legs. Yet Jack was able to perform the hard physical work on the farm, to play tennis and other games for much of his adult life. The doctors were astonished. They did not know the intestinal fortitude of William John Duffell.

His son, John, and daughter, Gwendalyn, remember with affection a genial, nuggety little man, forever with a pipe in his mouth, and prone to thoughtful moods at times.

He had a lively sense of humour and loved playing harmless practical jokes on his family. And he loved airing his smattering of soldier Anglo-French phrases (expressed here with phonetic spelling). He would suddenly come out with 'Bon jour, mademoiselle Gwendalyn', 'ouvre la door', 'merci beaucoup', 'chercher la femme', 'aprez vous, madame', 'a mois, mes infants', 'come here, toot sweet Jaques'—all delivered with appropriate and exaggerated Gallic gestures and flourishes. Everything was either 'bon', 'par bon' or in army slang 'napoo'.

His granddaughter, Sylvia Allen, remembers him and Gleneta for the comical practical jokes, the tennis parties, the barn dances and fishing on the river. And the family singsongs around the piano at night, with ex-Gunner Duffell beefing out 'Mademoiselle from Armentières' with great gusto.

And yet in other ways Jack Duffell was a stern disciplinarian of the military mould. Table manners were strictly enforced. No elbows on the table, stand up when Mother comes into the room, don't speak with your mouth full. But this did nothing to destroy his main role as a loving and caring father.

An avid reader of books, with a preference for history, facts and figures, and anything to do with the war, he read himself to sleep at night and always had a book propped up in front of him at breakfast. He kept all kinds of diaries and notes about farm management and John, junior, remembers the winter his father began to write his 25,000-word account of his war, based on his daily diaries and letters home. There he was, a pipe in his mouth, sitting in front of the fire in the big armchair he had made himself, a writing pad on his knee. He wrote it in ink in longhand, a little each night until it was finished.

Farmer Duffell was back in uniform again in World War II. He served as a captain in the VDC (Volunteer Defence Corps) and was manpower officer of the Griffith district.

It all caught up with him about the year 1960 when he was sixty-three. His heart was playing up more often and his legs were so bad that he had difficulty in walking. They bought a 'shooting stick' for him to get around with and the Repatriation Department at last classified him as TPI (Totally and Permanently Incapacitated). This entitled him to a liberal service pension.

He sold Gleneta and retired to a house in Griffith. There he died suddenly on 23 May 1966, at the age of sixty-nine.

The funeral of William John Duffell was one of the biggest and most impressive Griffith had ever seen, with a police escort. The *Griffith Times* described him as 'a man of insight and civic pride who would be remembered as ever in readiness to extend a helping hand in time of need'. It was recalled that he had founded the first Yenda Diggers' Club, with Angus Moore, had been president of the Yenda RSL Club for nine years, and been a director of the Yenda Producers' Co-op and many other local organisations.

Maybe in his later years, Gunner Duffell might have wondered how on earth a seventeen-year-old Hurstville kid had managed to get caught up with such a momentous and horrendous thing as a world war and leave a record of it behind in 153 letters home.

His epitaph was most surely written by himself in describing his return to Australia in 1918: 'Thus ended the service of one who served to the best of his ability'.

Postscript

Just to tidy things up a bit, this is what happened to the main characters in this book.

Gunner Duffell's father and mother, William and Lucy Duffell, paid many visits to the farm at Yenda. William spent his last years there after the death of his wife.

Mary Dircks died in Griffith barely two years after the loss of her beloved husband.

Lilian (Sis) married a banker.

Henry (Bro), the juvenile terror of Hurstville, grew up into a quiet and good-natured real estate agent in Cronulla.

Cassie Harris, the 'little Welch girl', never came to Australia. She married an engineer named Jack Farrell, and died in 1970. There were no children. Her sister Beatie never married and died in 1980, aged ninety. Their mother, Jack Duffell's 'second mother', died in 1960.

Another matter requiring elucidation concerns the small diary of a dead German soldier retrieved from his body by Gunner Duffell in a trench in Flanders. John Duffell said it was his father's dearest wish that the diary be returned one day to the German soldier's remaining family, and efforts are being made to do so.

The diary has a picture of Kaiser Wilhelm on the cover. The only clues to the identity of the owner are the initials R.L. and the fact that he was a draughtsman with a firm of architects in Frankfurt-on-Main.

A friend of the Duffell family, Jimmy Ronaldson, has translated the diary, which tells of the young soldier's induction into the German Army and his training. On 6 May 1917, the young soldier wrote of his past: 'At the beginning of this war I was at Frankfurt-on-Main employed by Schaffiner and Albert in the architects' office as a draughtsman. There was almost nothing for me to do so I followed willingly the call of Uncle Adolf to help him in his printery.'

A feature of the diary is the description of a recurring dream which foretold the young soldier's death in most unusual detail.

Jimmy Ronaldson says he appeared to have not been more than twenty in 1914 when he joined the German Army. He became a corporal and fought in the great Battle of Verdun:

After Verdun, he must have landed in hospital in 1917 when he got this notebook for a diary and started to recapitulate his experiences to date. From hospital I guess he went to machine-gun school and used the book for notes on the M.G., having dropped the idea of a diary. By the date, you will see that the Dream was written at the same time as he started the diary and was evidently a direct result of his experiences at Verdun. Of the pieces of verse in the diary, there are well-known songs and some unknown to me.

Appendix

The Duffell Diaries

Gunner Duffell kept three small pocket diaries throughout his service overseas. His first entry was made on 1 January 1916, at sea between Australia and Egypt, and the last on 5 October 1918, on arrival home at Sydney. He made an entry every day, under all circumstances. The diaries are in remarkably good condition, considering he must have written them at times while in muddy dugouts with German shells screaming overhead. Here are some extracts.

1916

January 27 [Egypt]: Went on battery drill as brakesman. Team bolted & the lead driver thrown. Worked in horse lines. Had inspection by C.O. Fainted (sun).

March 20 [Egypt]: Travelled all night embarked 8 a.m. on the Knight Templar. Lost horse overboard. Sailed 6 p.m. for unknown.

March 28 [France]: Arrived Marseilles. Marched 10 miles to camp. Slept in old mill house. Very cold. French people very hospitable & obliging.

April 6: Rained all day. Mud a foot thick everywhere. Vaccinated again for 3rd time.

May 13: In action at last. Very quiet in morning. Plenty of action afternoon.

October 20: Payed. Half Battery drunk. Spent evening in village, had good time. Terrible cold.

October 21: Resting all day, ready to move off midnight. Half the battery drunk again.

October 22: Left at 1.30 a.m. Travelled 7 miles to Audruicq entrained for 12 hours. Detrained Amiens.

October 30: Lieut Holmes wounded seriously. Still raining. Horses dying of exposure.

November 11: Stunts all day. Fritz counter attacks stopped. Saw Taube brought down in flames.

November 13: Fritz shelled all round us all night & this morning.

November 14: Everything iced over. Frost like snow. Taubes over saw grand fights 3 taubes down.

December 25: Went to high mass in Amiens Cathedral. strange but interesting.

1917

March 24: Still resting in village. Finished work early & spent rest of day reading & dodging Officers & N.C.O.'s.

May 26: Put on gun guard 24 hours. Two drunks put in guard tent. Had swim.

August 16: Opened fire with heavy barrage 4.45 a.m. Tommies advanced 2000 yds but were pushed back to original line during day. Fired 900 odd rounds per gun. Aircraft in action all day. Saw 2 huns & 1 ours brought down. Two more killed up forward.

August 29: Still raining & cold. Spent day cleaning up position. Put crosses on graves of the boys killed.

June 15: Fritz started shelling after dinner & put about 200 shells over. Not much damage. Gas attack on but gas blown away from here.

July 24: Pozieres village taken. Still shelling hard. Inf have taken more trenches & prisoners. Terrible lot Aust wounded.

July 29: Shells falling through night & all day. Many more wounded.

Grand fight between hun aircraft & ours. Gas shells coming over but wind blowing wrong way to hurt us.

October 10: Still raining & winds. Sent up to guns as layer. Fritz shelled all night. Dug out knocked in & six men buried.

October 30: All day Fritz sent heavy stuff over our position. More gas shells over.

October 31: [The diary gives this as the night Gunner Duffell was gassed; in his later account he makes it November 2] Fritz still hammering away at our position. At night he sent gas over for some hours. Feeling bad.

November 1: Sent to WL feeling effects of last nights gas.

November 3: Not feeling too bright. Taube over. Brought down by machine guns.

November 7: Not feeling too bright. Doctor marked me for England, very cold & wet outside. Expect to go tomorrow.

December 25 [Wales]: Had usual quiet Xmas. After good dinner went to organ recital.

December 27: Spent day walking about mountains with girls. Had musical evening. Had fortune told.

1918

The 1918 diary, during Jack's convalescence and inactivity at Hurdcott, was full of such phrases at 'still raining', 'still snowing', 'nothing doing all day' and 'wrote letters'.

January 9: Freezing all day. Mooched about morning & afternoon.

January 25: On fatigue duty all day. Head giving me trouble, aching every day.

March 15: Worked in bread store all day. Heart giving a good deal of trouble.

April 5: Nothing doing in barbers saloon. Raining.

May 13: On medical board morning. Marked C1 [Home service England].

June 15 [Westham Camp]: Went to town evening. Aussies Yank tars & Jacks mixed matters. Win for us.

June 23: Went to church morning. Spent afternoon & evening in Weymouth. Went walking over cliffs with E.J. [his 'little Dorset girl'?].

July 15: Torpedoed by Hun U boat 5 p.m. 260 miles from land. Took to boats & was picked up by destroyers. Submarine sunk by depth charges.

August 23 [SS *Carpentaria* in Sierra Leone]: Pretty place. Natives came around ship in canoes selling fruit etc.

August 26: Blowing a gale. Heavy seas running. Heat bad.

August 27: Still blowing with heavy sea. Played cards & read etc.

August 28: Over the line. Father Neptune comes aboard with wife & staff. Calmer today.

September 2: Ship rolled a lot. Wind dying down. Getting cooler every day. Good war news though. Boys doing good work.

September 4: Still rough. Head & heart affected. Nothing to do.

October 5: Halted for breakfast at Moss Vale. Arrived Sydney 10 a.m. Taken to Buffet in motor cars. Met people & came home in car. Great welcome.

Bibliography

Only a few basic sources of information were consulted as background for Duffell's letters. No attempt has been made to analyse or pass judgment on the battles or generals and politicians who directed them:

Australian Encyclopaedia, Australian Geographic Society.
Bean, C.E.B., *Official History of Australian in the War of 1914-18*, Angus & Robertson.
Colliers Encyclopaedia, Macmillan Education Co.
Encyclopaedia Britannica.
Gibbs, Philip, *The Battles of the Somme*, William Heinemann.
Hart, B.H. Liddell, *History of the First World War*, Pan Books.
Robson, L.L., *The First A.I.F.*, Melbourne University Press.
Sixsmith, E.K.G., *Douglas Haig*, Weidenfield and Nicolson.

Special thanks are due to the Duffell Family; Hastings Municipal Library, Port Macquarie; Hurstville Municipal Council; Neil McDonald; Gerard Thompson; Yvonne Bartlett Hawes; and Mrs Peggie Lowe, Skewen, South Wales.

Index

19th Battalion, 82
1st Australian Field Artillery
    Brigade, 25, 113
    13th Reinforcements, 15
3rd Army, British, 81
4th Division, Australian, 81
Anzac Buffet in the Domain,
    147
Anzac Corps, 49
Anzac Ridge, 113
Arabia, 66
Armistice, 148
Artillery
    Australian, 58
    problems with moving, 78–9
Audruicq, 157
Bapaume, 81
Barunga, SS, sinking of, 135–41
Bean, C.E.W., 69, 113
Behencourt, 77, 79, 80, 83–4
Berrima, SS, 15–19, 21–3
    Xmas at sea, 17, 18
    rioting of 'Berrima boys' in
        Perth, 19–21
    shipboard life, 17, 18, 22–4
Biscay, Bay of, 136
Blackboy Hill military camp,
    breakout at, 19–21
Blackpool, 88–9

Blighty, origin of word, 86
Boulogne, convalescent camp at,
    37
British Expeditionary Force, 34
Bullecourt, Allied assault on,
    82–3
Burrinjuk Reservoir, 149
Cairo, 26–7, 29
Calais, Lahore British General
    Hospital at, 36–7
Cape Town, riot at, 144
Carpentaria, SS, 143–6, 159
Chifley, Ben, 104
Chlorine gas attacks, 33, 112–13
Conscription, 127, 130, 133
    referendum, 61–2
    second referendum, 123
Darcy, Les, 103–4
Death penalty, under the
    Australian Defence Act, 62
Delville Wood, 60
Depression of the 1930s, 151
Desertion, death penalty for, 62
Despatch work, 38, 39
Dircks, Mary (Mollie), 11, 12,
    47, 85, 107, 109, 131, 144,
    147, 149–52, 154
    marriage to John Duffell, 151
Dorman, Bert, 109

Duffell ancestry in Australia, 10, 11

Duffell, Gwendalyn, 151

Duffell, Haroldl ('Tommy'), 42, 80-1

Duffell, Lucy Elena, 13, 42, 154

Duffell, Roy, 151

Duffell, Thomas John, 151

Duffell, William Thomas, 13, 42, 154

Egypt, 25-9, 156

Etaples Base Hospital, 115

Financial worries, 72

Flanders Campaign, The, 89

Flers, 61

Fletcher, Perce, 66

Food, 45, 46, 77

France, arrival of the Australians in, 31

Fremantle, 146

Frostbite, 77

Gallagher, Major, 20

Gallipoli campaign, 14
   Australian divisions withdrawn from, 25

Gas attacks, 33, 51, 96, 112-13, 115

Gibbs, Sir Philip, 48

Gleneta, 151-2

Griffith Soldier Settlers Memorial, 152

Haig, General Sir Douglas (later Field Marshal), 33, 47, 69, 95, 126

Hamel, capture of the sector, 133

Harefield Park, Australian auxiliary hospital at, 117, 119

Harris family, 88, 143

Harris, Beatie, 88, 143, 154

Harris, Cassie, 43, 88, 91, 123, 143, 154

Harris, Jack, 86-9, 98-9, 109, 130

Harris, Mrs, 122-4, 127, 143, 154

Hart, Sir Basil H. Liddell, 49, 50, 95, 113

Hazebrouck, 37-8

Heliopolis, 26

Hellfire Corner, 101

Highwood, 77

Hindenburg Line, The, 81

Holmes, Lieutenant, 157

Honour boards, 85, 131

Horse handling, 26

Hughes, W.M. (Billy), 61, 130

Hunter, Sergeant Ted, 139

Hurdcott, convalescent wards at, 117, 121, 123, 158

Kent (cruiser), 136, 137

Kitchener, General Lord, 25

La Boiselle, 56

La Vallentine, 32

Lance (destroyer), 137, 142

Le Havre, camp near, 35

Lice, 45, 46, 66

London, 86, 87

Loos, Battle of, gas used as a weapon at, 112

Luck, Peter, 103

Lusitania, sinking of, 14

Mametz Wood, 57

Marseille, 32, 156

Messines, 89
   Battle of, 105

Middlesex War Hospital, 116, 119

Midge (destroyer), 137, 142

Minneapolis, SS, sinking of, 31

Moore, Angus, 153

Murrumbidgee Irrigation Area, 149, 151

Mustard gas attacks, 96, 112-13

Mustard gas, effects of, 115, 129

NSW Water Conservation and Irrigation Commission, 150

Parcels, problems with, 103

Paris, 126
Passchendaele, 95–115
  the bombardment at, 96
  the swamps of, 96
  the village, 96
Plymouth, 142
Polson, John, 16, 102
Poperinghe, field hospital at,
  115, 118
Pozieres
  fighting near, 44
  taken by Australian troops,
  54
Prisoners, German, 79, 83, 89,
  100
Rainville, 27
Red Lodge, 105
Red Sea, 23
Reveille (RSL magazine),
  150
Rioting
  of 'Berrima' boys in Perth,
  19–21
  between 3rd and 4th
  Divisions, 89
  between Australian soldiers
  and American sailors, 135
  at Cape Town, 144
Riverina, 150
Ronaldson, Jimmy, 154
Russia, 125
Russian Revolution, 80
SOS and gas guard, 99
Salvation Army, 142
Sausage Gully, 44, 56, 57
Sierra Leone, 159
Sixsmith, E.K.G., 64
Skewen, 88, 122, 123
Soldier settlement, 149, 150

Somme, The Battle of the, 33,
  49–64
  bombardment of German
  positions at, 47–8
  cost in lives, 49
  weather, 69–72, 77–8
Souvenirs of war, 87
Strikes in Australia, 104, 109
Submarine attack on SS
  Barunga, 135–41
Suez Canal, Turko-German
  threat to, 25
Swanson, Laura, 16
Tel el Kebir, camp at, 27
Tommies (British soldiers), 127
Toulon, 31
Trench life, 45
Verdun, defence of, 34
Victory (destroyer), 137, 142
Villers-Bretonneux, 127
Volunteer Defence Corps,
  Duffell's service in, 153
Western Front, 34
Westham Camp in Dorset, 127,
  134, 142, 158
Weymouth, 135, 142
Wilton Hotel, London, 86–7
Wiltshire, army convalescent
  camp in, 125–6
YMCA, 142
Yenda, the farm at, 108, 150–4
Ypres, 52
  Third Battle of, *see*
  Passchendaele
  attacks near, 96
  gas attack at, 112
  town of, 100
Zeitoun Military Camp,
  Heliopolis, 25–9